New Life, No Instructions

Center Point
Large Print

**This Large Print Book carries the
Seal of Approval of N.A.V.H.**

New Life, No Instructions

a memoir

GAIL CALDWELL

CENTER POINT LARGE PRINT
THORNDIKE, MAINE

This Center Point Large Print edition is published in the
year 2014 by arrangement with Random House,
an imprint of Random House,
a division of Random House LLC.

The text of this Large Print edition is unabridged.
In other aspects, this book may vary
from the original edition.
Printed in the United States of America
on permanent paper.
Set in 16-point Times New Roman type.

ISBN: 978-1-62899-095-9

Library of Congress Cataloging-in-Publication Data

Caldwell, Gail, 1951–
New life, no instructions : a memoir / Gail Caldwell. —
    Center Point Large Print edition.
pages ; cm
ISBN 978-1-62899-095-9 (library binding : alk. paper)
1. Caldwell, Gail, 1951– 2. Journalists—United States—Biography.
    3. Critics—United States—Biography.
    4. Total hip replacement—Patients—Biography.
    5. Large type books. I. Title.
PN4874.C2187A3 2014
070.92—dc23
[B]
                                                    2014003990

For Dick Chasin

"[But] it's no use going back to yesterday, because I was a different person then."

—Lewis Carroll,
Alice's Adventures in Wonderland

I wonder about the pilgrims at Lourdes and Fátima, the ones who felt the glow and realized they could walk. Was it pure ecstasy from the get-go, or something gradual—doubt turning into hope, then joy? Did they hesitate at all? Maybe they were a little skeptical: *OK, so I can walk again, but I should keep the crutches just in case . . .*

Grace or hallucination, their encounters gave them something, even a simple dose of courage. The real task must have come later, after they absorbed what had happened: miracle, new life, no instructions.

New Life,
No Instructions

1.

....

Cambridge 2011

My first tip-off that the world had shifted was that the dogs looked lower to the ground. I dismissed the perception as a visual misread: Because I was on crutches and couldn't bend down to touch them, of course they would seem farther away. Then a friend came to visit, a striking woman whom I'd always considered tall. She was standing across the living room and I was smiling, happy to have her there, and I thought, *Tink is small! And I never realized it before.*

The fact is that Tink is about my size, but until that day I had looked up to her in more ways than one. I was just home from five days at New England Baptist Hospital, where the chief of joint reconstruction had built me a new hip and lengthened my right leg by five-eighths of an inch. The measurement sounds deceptively slight, but then pi, unexplained, doesn't mean much, either. What the extended hip bought me was about two inches of additional height, because I was no longer bending forward in pain. It gave my leg something immeasurable: an ability to reach the ground, and the chance and anatomical equipment to walk right for the first time in my life.

Almost as dramatic, at least in the beginning, was the reorientation of my physical self in space. My perspective had been jolted to the point that trees and cars and other markers of street life felt closer to me, within reach in a way they hadn't before. I could sense the effort involved in making these neural adjustments: In a simple movement like a step forward, particularly outside, there would be a lurch of visual confusion, then acceptance. It happened quickly and brilliantly, and my comprehending it changed everything: What had seemed to be mere dizziness was in fact the brain's ballet.

These were transient phenomena, the brain being a nimble choreographer of time and space. Within a few weeks I would be accustomed to the additional height and leg length; our bodies, perfect feats of design, respond to what is in front of them, usually without even bothering to let us know. But the dance I found myself doing with the physical world in the first few days and weeks after surgery signaled something larger, more long-lasting, that I would have to learn and relearn in the following year: the notion that life has an agency, some will and forward motion, greater than one's own wish or intention. *The force that through the green fuse drives the flower,* Dylan Thomas called it. The idea that the whole blessed shebang doesn't have to be a free fall after all.

I caught polio when I was six months old, in 1951, during one of the last years of the U.S. epidemic, before the vaccines. The virus, which destroys neurons, can lead to full or partial permanent paralysis; it affected the muscles in my right leg, and I didn't walk until I was past the age of two. Still, the mark on my family's door was relatively faint: no March of Dimes crutches or iron lung, just a faltering leg that often went unnoticed. The fact of the disease—important but hardly central—had long been incorporated into my shorthand self-description: writer, grew up in Texas, slight limp from polio. Part of the story I'd told myself all my life was that polio had made me a fighter—that I was hellbent on being strong because of it—and that much was still true. But in the past few years, within the joys and demands of raising a young dog, I had begun to experience pain and lameness I'd never known before. The mystery of this decline cast a shroud of defeat over what I feared lay ahead. It seemed that the aftereffects of the disease had reemerged, ghostly and conniving, like a stalker who'd never left town.

And then: A standard X-ray, ordered probably fifteen years after it was called for, revealed that the scaffolding of my hip was a junkyard of bone. However compromised my leg had been by polio, muscles can't work without a structure to hold them up. That I had been walking around at all, I was told, was astounding—and a lot of my recent decline could be addressed by one of the most common surgeries in modern medicine. The rest—the retraining and possible strengthening of a rebuilt leg—would be up to me.

What do you do when the story changes in mid-life? When a tale you have told yourself turns out to be a little untrue, just enough to throw the world off-kilter? It's like leaving the train at the wrong stop: You are still you, but in a new place, there by accident or grace, and you will need your wits about you to proceed.

The revelation that there was a medical solution before me—a high-tech fix to pain and infirmity that by now seemed endemic and existential—shifted the angle of my vision in some essential way. It opened up the future and tinted the past, in the way that the unexpected can always disarm the reach of yesterday. Despite the mind-over-matter stoicism of Western thought, the mind cannot grasp the concept of wellness until the body announces it. The idea that I would some-how and someday be able to walk better—to walk without pain or urgent concentration—was a foreign notion and required a leap of faith. I didn't really believe it until months after surgery, when I saw my right foot climb a stair without asking my brain for permission first. I was being offered a new chapter to an old story, and the beginning of something else altogether.

This rearranging of a life started out, too, as a love story—a human-canine one, filled with the usual pratfalls and dropped cues of romance. My four-legged Boswell was a young Samoyed named Tula, a beautiful, irascible sled dog with an intrepid heart and the strength of a tractor. Trying to keep up with her—trying to be a middle-aged athlete in a failing body—was what first revealed to me the sort of trouble I was in. As she hurled herself through life with me stumbling along behind, she became my divining rod, herding me toward places I could not have gone alone.

She stood by when I fell and got up and tried again; accordingly, I tried to pay attention to the world as she saw it. Dogs have a present-tense alacrity that makes short shrift of yesterday's bad news. They are hard-wired to charge forth, to expect good outcomes, and that viewpoint can shape the future as much as it anticipates it. I don't believe I'd have staggered into this glen of insight and physical change without her.

· · ·

"Your body has been through a major trauma," a resident told me when I called the hospital at midnight, with a 100-degree fever and a racing heart. "It was a carefully controlled trauma, but it's still a trauma." It was my first night home, several days after surgery, and I'd been told to report any signs of fever or shortness of breath. The surgical fellow who answered my call sounded sleepy but interested. I said I'd been released from the hospital that afternoon and gave him all my vital stats—blood pressure, hematocrit, oxygen levels, history of trans-fusions.

"You're lucid and articulate," he said. "I know that doesn't matter much to you right now, but it matters greatly to me."

I realized that he meant I wasn't raging with fever or non compos mentis from infection. "Your symptoms are distressing to you but not dangerous," he said. "They're all completely within the realm of normal."

"In other words," I said, "a bulldozer just ran over me, but the guy driving knew what he was doing?"

"Exactly!" he said, and we both laughed, and both, or so I assumed, went back to sleep.

Days of inpatient physical therapy had taught me how to maneuver the crutches I would be on for the next six weeks. My house was full of friends and food and as prepped as a military canteen. But when I first got inside the door, all I could see was the obstacle course that lay before me: all those stairs and chairs and corners and narrow paths. I had been reduced to the most elemental part of being human: living utterly in the physical world. Even through the blur of painkillers, I was not much more than a set of sensate responses to pain—pain being a self-contained universe, not so much awful as it was all-consuming. For what seems like forever but was probably a week or less, I lived only according to its dictates.

"Do people ever regret having this surgery?" I was pleasant enough when I asked this question of my physical therapist, who came to my house the next morning. But I was dead serious. I felt mauled. Worse, I was afraid I had allowed myself to be mauled—that something horrid and ineradicable had transpired from which I would never recover. The physical therapist was chipper and gracious and she didn't hesitate to answer. "Oh yes!" she said, and I flinched. Then she said, "Most of them are where you are right now. At the end of the tunnel, they say it changed their life."

"How long is the tunnel?" I asked.

"About six months," she said.

"And how long is the horrible part?" I said.

This time she paused. "About four weeks."

OK, I thought. I can do four weeks of horrible, to change a life.

My history with polio and my parents' reaction to it—my mother's early fortitude, my father's rough-bluster loyalty—are what first tempted me to gather this narrative, to splice past into present and try to make sense of it all. Polio is a far greater medical odyssey than my experience can even hint at; its individual stories are in danger of being forgotten as a piece of the social tapestry, because its firsthand witnesses, at least in the developed West, are middle-aged or older.

Most of all I told this story because I wanted to say something about hope and the absence of it, and how we keep going anyway. About second chances, and how they're sometimes buried amid the dross, even when you're poised for the down-hill grade. The narrative can always turn out to be a different story from what you expected.

Hope isn't my long suit, but if momentum is a physical version of hope, well, I've got that. I still have dreams of crawling as an infant, and my body heaves in an absolute sense of going forward, with a kind of determination that feels like rushing water; it is the way one throws off despair. As long as I can keep moving in the dream, I am all right. So I wanted to tell people that—to say that sometimes force is all you have, and that has to be enough. Because with just that force, according to Newton, eventually you get to someplace else. A calculus of hope and motion.

There's a term in scientific language, vast and precise, that came into being after Einstein changed everything: *slower than the speed of light.* That's me—that's the ordinary world—and I'll take it.

2.

....

Winter in the Texas Panhandle, sometime in the mid-1950s. My sister, Pam, who was two years older, had already left for school, so I must have been about four. I was lying on the carpeted floor of our living room, in a small house in Amarillo, next to my mother. We were in our robes and pajamas, the grate from the floor furnace warming us nearby, and we were doing foot walks up and down the wall. I can still see the pale-green color of the room and the dark wooden front door, which I stared at while we did my exercises. Nothing hurt that I can recall, but I remember a physical frustration so utter that, in the child's universe, it was assumed. When I got tired, I started to complain. "Just a few more, honey," my mother would unfailingly say. "Here, I'll do them with you." And up and down we'd go, wall walks and then leg lifts and upright toe raises, with me holding on to her wrists while I tried—mostly futilely—to walk on my heels.

The memory of this daily regimen is coarse, more atmospheric than chronological, and it overrides most of my earliest memories. Decades later, I asked my mother how long we spent on the floor together. "Oh, about two hours a day, I guess," she said. "For three or four years."

I was one of the tens of thousands hit by polio in the summer of 1951, part of the last wave of casualties before the massive Salk vaccine trials began in 1954. National panic closed the public swimming pools and had parents trying to guard their children from an enemy they couldn't see. A highly infectious virus that affects the central nervous system, polio can range in severity from a negligible fever to a ravaging illness with lethal results. Though the virus can lead to permanent muscle damage or paralysis, the majority of those infected recover completely.

Mine was a mild enough case to be misdiagnosed for years. "You were just burning up," my mother remembered. "And I'd put you there on a quilt in the living room so I could watch you, and you'd just lie there—you were so weak." But I was too young to manifest any blatant signs, like falling down, which would have been clear in an older child, too young to articulate the telltale fatigue and muscle cramps and weakness that were a signature of the disease. The doctors thought I had a bad virus—fever of more than 104 for weeks on end—and when it finally dissipated on its own, no one thought anything else about it.

Until I didn't walk, and didn't walk. I crawled

for the next two years. Amarillo in the 1950s was not, say, Mass General, and the pediatrician told my mother, "Oh, she'll walk when she's ready." My mother told me this throughout my life, especially when I was an adult, when we were trying to untangle what had happened and whether anything might have been done about it. "You would grab on to that coffee table in the living room," she told me, "and you'd hoist yourself up and try to stand. Then you'd plop down onto the carpet and sit there for a minute, and then you'd try again."

My mother always relayed these stories with a mix of wistfulness and affection, as though she remembered the efforts of the child she loved as well as the continual failure. In the spring of 1953, she had to go into the hospital for something minor, and her sister Dorothy came to take care of Pam and me. "Dorothy said, 'When you get out of the hospital I'm going to have that child walking,' " my mother remembered, then paused for a split second. "But she didn't."

There was just a trace of competitiveness in this recitation, the mother claiming primacy, as though she couldn't bear to have her sister claim that victory—to be the first to see the child walk—when she herself could not.

More than five decades later, what startles me is the fierceness of my own memory, of trying to get up and stay there. Some of it is visual—the color of the carpet, which was never too far away, the layout of the living room from where I sat on the floor, and how much the world expanded when I raised myself up. And so I have to believe it is a true memory, not just the imagined one from listening to my mother's stories. Mostly my recall is physical, and larger than my own body: the feeling of force bumping up against mass, time and time again, and mass always winning. It is a sadder memory to me now than it must have been at the time, because the child's world is finite until we break through it with motion. We can't yet imagine where we haven't been. I do feel it as a solitary event, as though my young body and mind grasped that I had to do this myself. And I think the collision of my momentum with my limitations was confusing. We are engineered to rise up, in every developmental sense. Normally a child walks somewhere between twelve and eighteen months, at which point her environment explodes into possibility. The brain and heart are ready to seize everything within reach.

I don't remember my first step, or the consciousness shift from crawling to walking, which came when I was two and a half years old. I have no idea if this lurch into a higher, upright world was painful or thrilling or anywhere in between, but once I was up, I found a way to make it work. Apparently I slung out my right leg—the one afflicted—ahead of me and to the side, like Chester on *Gunsmoke*, using it as a sort of pivot to launch my stronger leg forward. It's a physical gesture that my leg, holder of muscle memories conscious and unconscious, will still duplicate when I am tired.

My sister was a tomboy, the movable object that whirled around me. Adoring and ever complicit, I was her willing sidekick, partly because she had access to the locomotive of life that I limped along behind.

"What do you remember about the polio?" I asked her recently.

"Nothing," she said, no hesitation in her voice. Then, after a pause: "It was just always there, like the air."

That in itself gives it a more vivid place in consciousness than I retain: Like a well patient viewing the one in the hospital bed, Pam saw a different reality from the one I perceived. If I recognized the force field of my own constraints, I remember just as clearly the things I mastered: I learned to swim when I was about four, and loved it so thoroughly that I had to be extracted from the pool. You could swim outside in the Panhandle from April to October, and four or five days a week in summer my mother drove us to the Western Riviera swim club, a place of ease and chlorine and sunbaked perfection. When Pam and I went diving for pennies, I held my breath for so long that I repeatedly alarmed the lifeguards.

For years I fantasized about being a mermaid: my imaginary, Olympian life of easy movement. And I remember synchronized swimming with a delirious, out-of-time pleasure that my body still responds to: flip, arms spread, feet kicking, the other girls in perfect (or so it seemed) harmony around me. The lights were on in the pool: Was this a nighttime performance, little girls giving their dance recital in the water? It was the era of Esther Williams, the Hollywood swimmer with the chin-strap cap and dazzling smile, mugging for the camera while petals of swimmers unfolded around her with military grace. So my recollection of this event is probably mixed up with my imagined want of it. But I know it was the one activity I could do that my sister could not, and that the water itself—sweet and infinite shelter—was a place where all legs were created equal, where balance wasn't mandatory and no cruel ground or gravity reached up to stop me. Impossible to fall down in the water.

My dad used to say that bluff can carry you a long way. Here are the things I could not do as a kid: ride a bike, jump rope, run track, play softball or basketball. Here's the more important thing: I'm not sure how much I cared. I do remember feeling relief when my parents decided I didn't have to try anymore to keep a two-wheeler upright. But as that door closed, other corridors revealed themselves. I read after bedtime in the closet with a flashlight. I learned fractions from my dad by looking over his shoulder at his beloved stock pages in the newspaper. He took me quail- and dove-hunting in the empty wilds outside of Amarillo, and taught me to fish off the long pier at Port Aransas, on the Texas Gulf. There is even a picture of me, age four, on a horse one summer in Colorado—though the other three members of my mounted family are grinning, and I am clutching the saddle horn on my enormous old horse, stricken, looking as though I've been grabbed by King Kong.

Most of my bad memories about polio and its effects involve the orthopedic surgeon we saw, a cold, unfriendly man with a mustache whom I must have demonized. He poked and prodded; he declared me lazy when I didn't walk by age two. At some point he put me in heavy orthopedic shoes, horrid tie-up oxfords, which I wore to school and then promptly stashed in my locker, exchanging them for a pair of girlish flats I had hidden there. The last time I remember seeing him, when I was eight or nine, he used a reflex hammer too roughly on my knee to test my response, and when my leg popped up, I intentionally kicked him in the chin.

This was atypical. I was a mild-mannered girl until adolescence, but I was already stubborn, and I had clearly had enough of this doctor. I don't mean to downplay the psychological effects of polio or succumb to the tough persona that, for better and worse, I cultivated through a lot of life. The truth is that I felt a terrible impotence when my leg failed me, when it was put to the test in athletics, and I struggled mightily to create as many other paths as possible. And I set out to avoid failure at almost any cost.

I hit adolescence in the early 1960s, pre–Title IX, when girls' athletics were neglected and even perceived as uncool, and somehow my resilience and my body type gave me a way out. I shot up four inches in a year, and so became a gangly girl who walked a bit crookedly. When my friends ran for cheerleader, I ran for student council; while they were doing pyramids and flips on the football field, I buried myself in algebra and edited the high school annual. We went on a class skiing trip to Ruidoso, New Mexico, and when I promptly fell down on the bunny slope, the boys started calling me "Grace," a friendly, half-flattering nickname that stuck through adolescence.

As with most blueprints of a life, my internal circumstances conspired with history to create an imperfect and complex essence: ungainly but leggy, unathletic but class clown, smart but rebellious. I spent a lot of time mouthing off in class or smoking in the parking lot. The rebellion was typical; the degree of it was not. I was like a half-lame horse trying to get out of the gate: frustrated and anxious and mad with desire. I turned some of that initial impotence into fury and determination, despair doing a head race with blind will.

And somewhere, always, is my mother, the valiant coach on the floor beside me. The woman who, well into her seventies, went with me to the town swimming pool whenever I visited Amarillo. She took a seat on the bleachers and watched me swim laps for a half hour or longer, which I had begun doing in my twenties and have done ever since. In keeping with the general sparseness of the Panhandle, I was usually the only one in the pool. She was the sole spectator, no book or magazine to distract her, and when I emerged from a flip turn and looked her way, she would smile and wave. As though there were nothing more fascinating than watching a grown daughter slice through the water, stroke after stroke, for laps on end, in a quiet pool. My intrepid, tinder-dry mother. Years after her death, it is one of my favorite memories of her.

3.

....

Both my parents had grown up on farms in East Texas, and had an easy way with animals. Every Easter we got take-out chicks and ducklings—a commonplace practice in Texas in the fifties. A week or two before the holiday, pastel chicks would appear in the garden centers, their feathers dyed green and pink and purple. My mom and dad preferred the natural variety; we usually brought home two or three hatchlings that quacked and chirped around our sunny backyard.

One year we brought home a pair of ducklings and named them Wadlington and Quack Quack, and my sister, who was four or five, got an early lesson in the perils of unrequited love. I got a lesson that was more subtle and probably formative.

Pam fell hard for Wadlington, who had already imprinted on my dad and followed him everywhere. Distraught over the duckling's inattention one day while she was playing, Pam cast Wadlington away from her, and he fell sideways off the back stoop and broke his leg.

My father was a tough and calm man, more

softhearted than he could ever display. First he consoled my sister, who was beside herself with hurt and regret. Then he went about fixing her mistake. He got a Popsicle stick and a roll of gauze, and soon the duck had a splinted leg and a cardboard box to recuperate in. Pam and my dad took care of Wadlington for weeks. After the leg was healed, we drove the duckling to Memory Gardens, a cemetery park in downtown Amarillo, and released him into the pond there, where he glided onto the waters with the other ducks. On land, he would always walk with a limp, but on the surface of the pond, he was fully restored, a duck among ducks. We went back to visit him for years.

For a long time this story seemed straightforward, a sweet glimpse of my dad. Decades later, a few years after his death, I realized the emotional framework it must have provided me. Despite the physical evidence of what polio had done to me, my father mostly acted as though it had never happened. My entire life, he displayed his fierce loyalty by refusing to believe that there was anything wrong with my leg—or that anything held me back beyond my own failure of will.

His denial was infuriating until I understood it. He couldn't bear the notion of my injury. He bought me handsome goatskin cowboy boots and saddle-soaped them every time I returned home to Texas, until his hands were too arthritic to brush the leather. When he was eighty-five and on a walker, he assumed I was strong enough to catch him if he fell, even though he was twice my size. Of all the doubts I have suffered in my life, even in the chaos of adolescence, his love for me was one of the things I never questioned. If he had no splint to help me navigate the world, he relied instead on straightforward faith. Believing in my strength would make it so.

I think about the Wadlington story when given the reminder—trying to conquer the icy sidewalks of New England, say, or swimming one more length in a pool or pond, where I am still more stable than on land. My father tried to hide his tender-heartedness with gruffness, but he was also bull-headed to the point of absurdity, determined as the duck he saved that day and the daughter he raised. Whatever I was able to glean from watching Wadlington's fall and rise, I know it provided two unshakable instructions: that my dad could fix things—that you could take a bad situation and make it better—and that a creature with a fragile leg could make her way, could swim the ponds and have a normal life.

4.

....

Rarely does the attainment of a childhood fantasy possess the purity of the original: Being an astronaut may sound pretty cool until you get to higher math and astrophysics. My most enduring fantasy, though, turned out to be bulletproof. It involved a white dog, who got larger in size as I got older, and its manifestation in adult life was as enriching as the little-girl dream.

When I was about three, I had a stuffed white dog I carried everywhere. I skipped over dolls entirely and went straight from stuffed animals to books: *The Yearling* and *The Call of the Wild* and *The Swiss Family Robinson.* I pored over the color illustrations of white dogs in the family encyclopedia, from West Highland terriers to Great Pyrenees, until the pages were creased and worn. My grail arrived when I was eleven, in the form of a paperback edition of *How to Raise and Train a Samoyed* that I still own. I found the book at a pet store and begged my mother to buy it for me. No matter that I had never seen a Samoyed, hot West Texas being no place for a long-haired northern sled dog. However nebulous the future is to a child, I had linked mine to the white dog I envisioned by my side. She was my Rosebud before she even existed.

Tula was my second Samoyed. She flew home with me in the summer of 2008, nine weeks old and eleven pounds of love and trouble, already charming her way through life when I took her through security at the Baltimore airport. Months earlier I had lost my first Sam, Clementine, who for thirteen years brought such sweetness and freedom to my life that I swore I would never be without a dog again.

Clementine's death was the last in a string of losses I had suffered over the previous six years. My closest friend, Caroline, had died in 2002 of lung cancer when she was forty-two. A year later my father died, the great oak tree fallen on the landscape. And my mother, even at ninety-one an edifice of wit and strength, had died in my arms in 2006.

For the next two years my heart felt like a bombed-out village. Clementine and I patrolled it together, and because she was aged and failing, I lived in a state of anticipatory sorrow, clinging to what I had left with her and knowing what was ahead. After she was gone, I wanted to lie down amid the rubble and stay there.

We do get up, of course, which seems a wonder. People stumble forth from whole-scale atrocities and personal tragedies and ordinary miseries and find a way to go to the store, talk to God, buy bulbs for the fall planting. And yet I sensed that I had not just been pummeled by death but reshaped by it, poised now at some crucial junction between darkness and endurance, which is the realist's version of hope. It seemed obvious that every gesture we make to waylay loss—a walk taken, a symphony heard or composed—was either a trick on death or a transient reprieve, and I felt so saddened from this insight that I didn't think I had much fight left in me. I remember trying to describe the state to friends and getting a smile of sympathetic, slightly vacant concern, as though they cared about but could not envision this forest where I had landed. I am trying not to generalize despair, I said, but I didn't mean I was depressed—I wanted to explain the color of the world now. My inner dialogue felt like a stage direction for Shakespeare's tragedies: *Exeunt, with a dead march.* Grief without hope is desolation, my therapist said to me one day, and I knew he was right and that I had to crawl out of where I was and somehow find a way to keep going. I needed the rambunctious miracle that would prove the lie.

That's a tall order for a puppy: rescue a human from an avalanche of grief, demonstrate daily the necessity of the forward march. Even Tula, one of the more confident dogs I have known, might have balked at the job.

Now I have a sense of how much desperation eclipsed my judgment: I was heartbroken, and determined to repair the heartbreak as soon as I could—or at least cauterize the wound. Choosing to do so with a puppy from one of the more head-strong (and strong) breeds may not have been the most cautious decision in the world. I had no idea, that first summer, the degree of physical decline that was ahead of me in the next few years. But then one never knows what's around the bend; that's one of the sweet deals and limitations of consciousness. Otherwise we'd have died off eons ago, victims of our own paralysis or recklessness. If we knew what was coming no one would ever leave the house, or we might drive over every available cliff, or simply lose our minds from worry. What a monster that would be, peering into the future.

And I doubt in my case that knowing would have made a whit of difference. I suspect I'd have just floored the gas pedal.

In the months after Clementine's death, I researched breeders and stared at online photos of Samoyed puppies, trying to find an image that would jump-start my heart. I spent a while contemplating a border collie instead of a Samoyed, which is a bit like choosing to date a flight pilot instead of a rodeo clown. Mostly, I sat on the back porch near the garden where Clemmie had liked to lie in the last few years, or wandered my house in aimless sorrow. I'm lucky I didn't wind up with a llama in the backyard.

The mind steered me toward what the heart required. In the late 1990s, I had been a regular visitor to New England's largest dog show, where I went to watch agility and obedience com-petitions as well as conformation. Usually I came home from these excursions and cooed over Clementine's unkempt beauty, telling her how lucky she was to have missed the cosmetic ordeals of a show dog. Then one winter I went to the dog show and saw a male Samoyed who took my breath away. Awaiting his turn in the ring, he was resting on a high platform, so majestic and calm he could have been a still life for the breed standard. I paid twelve dollars for the program just so I could find out where he came from, and I learned the breeder was a woman who lived on Long Island. It was 1997, and Clemmie was two years old, and I remember thinking that, while Long Island was more than a stone's throw from Boston, when the time came for my next Samoyed, I was going to find this woman and her dogs.

That majestic dog turned out to be Travis a.k.a. Am/Can Ch. Sanorka's Moonlite Trip t'Ren J BISS, and, eleven years later, I went looking for his breeder through the national breed club website. She had been breeding Samoyeds for nearly five decades and had recently moved to rural Pennsylvania. I wrote her and told her I remembered Travis from the Boston dog show; I included a long description of my experience with Samoyeds, a photo of Clementine and me on the beach, and two references from a veterinarian and a trainer. I knew the drill; I wanted to impress her before she had the chance to grill me.

Janice was old-school. I realized it the first time I talked to her on the phone, when she didn't try to push a dog on me. I knew it when I asked her some overly intense, searching question about how she knew something and she replied, simply, "Well, I've been doing this a long time." She did a breeding only every couple of years, and I managed, by serendipity, to locate her the week after a litter of four females and three males had been born. She had one female available; she would be keeping one herself for show. Her kennel was five hundred miles away, and she told me she wouldn't fly her dogs. And while a part of me thought I was crazy, I remembered that I had had this woman in the back of my mind for more than a decade. So I sent her a check to, as she put it, hold the bitch.

When the litter was just under six weeks old, I went to visit, to see what I was in for. I knew I would be coming back in two or three weeks, when the puppies were ready to go to their new homes, and mine would still be small enough to ride with me on the plane back. I flew to Baltimore, then I rented a car and drove across eastern Pennsylvania, through rolling country, visiting the old battlegrounds and the military cemetery. I had reserved a hotel room in the town square of Gettysburg, and after dinner I went for a late-night swim in the outdoor rooftop pool. Then I lay on the deck under the stars, thinking about my life. I was fifty-seven years old. I lived in a rambling old house in Cambridge surrounded by concentric circles of intimacy. To my surprise, and only some regret, I had never found anyone I wanted to marry. Too many creatures I loved were gone. The well-advertised fabulous fifties had been, for me, about sadness and soldiering through. The morning stretch had become a middle-aged groan; when I looked in the mirror, I saw the beginnings of my father's aged face. How in God's name had I gotten here?

One of the quiet profundities of aging is when you realize that this is an ordinary and very un-profound moment. Inside every aging person is the ageless, blinking mind, asking, *How did I get here?* There may be a former linebacker inside the elderly man being helped across the street; the eighty-five-year-old woman selecting two oranges at the grocery store used to be a dancer, or a lawyer, or hoisted her children up over her head when they were small. It helps to know this, I think, because it widens the future, humbles you before the sovereignty of time. More important, it makes you reach toward the soul inside the rattled elderly lady ahead of you in the checkout line. You can see all the corners of the map in your fifties, probably for the first time in life. You still get to shape some of it, and finally have the sense to know how. I knew that, whatever paths awaited me, I wanted to be staggering forth with a Samoyed at my side. Or rather, given their propensity for pulling, charging along ahead of me.

I still had every reason to believe I was up to the job. I had hints, but only hints, of a physical decline I believed was slow-moving, normal, and inevitable. My leg had always been prone to injury, though I'd counteracted some of that frailty with decades of swimming and rowing and dog-walking. As Clementine had aged, she preferred a leisurely amble to a two-hour romp, and I had set my pace in response to hers. Now I would need to amp it up again. I thought I remembered the demands a young dog would place on me, and I wanted to get her through her wild years as soon as I could. Then, or so I envisioned, we could slow down together.

The obvious question here, at least to me, is this: Why would a woman in her late fifties with a bum leg decide to get another sled dog, bred to pull a thousand pounds? I asked this of myself almost daily for Tula's first few years. Though the tenor of the question varied from wry to dismayed, my answers were consistent. Because I loved the breed and couldn't imagine the pallor of life without a Samoyed. Because I wasn't ready to give up: give up the notion that we can freeze time, give up the self-image of a strong, competent woman who could handle a big dog. Because I was convinced that I could make up in brainpower and devotion what I lacked in physical stamina. Or maybe I was just foolish and headstrong and chasing a dream past its expiration date. Maybe I was just the middle-aged guy going after the Porsche. But now I was doing laps in a hotel pool by moonlight in some little town in Pennsylvania, waiting to meet my newly arranged destiny.

5.

....

I drove the twenty miles to Janice's place, nervous and already happy. She lived on a winding, wooded road, and I turned in to a driveway marked by a small wooden sign with SANORKA etched upon it. At the end of the drive I saw a gorgeous young Samoyed in full extension behind a fence, springing like a top with enthusiasm. And I shook my head and started grinning and said out loud, "Oh, my God, I am so done."

Janice came outside to meet me in the driveway. She was a quiet, pleasant woman who had managed to have beds of flowering begonias within the vicinity of her dogs, as well as an elaborate system of inside and outside runs and kennels. I had come prepared to do temperament testing, to separate the girls and boys and see who approached me and who seemed shy or exuberant. I had squeaky toys and ribbons in my pocket, lures and props to ascertain sociability and prey drive and all the other traits I wanted to believe I could judge from a five- or six-week-old litter. I had a little notepad and pen. And then I got inside the run with the puppies, and everything in my arsenal of preparedness became irrelevant. I stopped trying to impress Janice with my knowledge. I just sat down on the wooden floor of the outside run and let the dogs sniff and whimper and bite my shoelaces and climb all over me, and then I looked up at her and said, "Well, there's not a dud in the bunch, is there?"

Janice's co-breeder, a woman named Carol, who owned the dam and lived a few miles away, came over to meet me, and patiently posed with every squirming puppy while I took pictures with my cell phone. Puppies are typically color-coded in a litter, like baby lambs, with a strip of red or pink or green on their ears. I watched them hopping around for a mesmerizing hour, trying to get a take on the quiet one, the talky one, the independent one. I had retained almost no information at the end of this, probably because my heart eclipsed whatever rational determinations my brain was attempting. I knew the sire was calm and beautiful and the dam was loath to leave Carol's side; these were good signs. Unwisely, I had taken to a quiet girl who whimpered, and when I picked her up, reinforcing the behavior, Carol rolled her eyes and said, "Well, *that* was the wrong thing to do." I liked Carol immediately; she was tough and straightforward. She had bred Pembroke Welsh corgis for years, then fallen for the deviltry and beauty of

Samoyeds and never looked back. "She's soft," she declared that day about the quiet girl. "She'll need to be socialized."

Janice was making her selection for pick of the litter when the pups were seven weeks old; I would find out after that who was available to me. "Don't fall in love with anyone," she warned me, flicking a tail and examining a chin every time she touched a pup. "In two days, they'll be entirely different dogs."

"I'm thirteen years older than I was last time around," I told her. "I want a female who is calm and attached."

She shrugged and said, "Well, that's the breed." I hugged her and Carol good-bye and headed back home to await my fate.

I spent the next several days mooning over Quiet Girl, my version of falling for a photograph on Match.com. Then I got the crucial email from Janice, her decision revealed in typical no-nonsense fashion. Quiet Girl was not even mentioned; the one person ahead of me had clearly fallen for her sleepyhead charms. "The pups available to you are Orange, Purple and Blue," Janice wrote. "Blue will never fit into the crate you have. I don't think Purple will be able to be contained in a crate that long. I think Orange might do the best in this situation. We had a dog club party at my house on Saturday and everyone fell for Orange and Red. I am keeping Red, so you will be getting second pick. Is this OK or do you want to chance taking one of the others and maybe not getting her on the plane?"

My heart started fluttering. I wrote back a long, torturous message about who Orange Girl was—I couldn't even remember her, just one of a movable mass of white cotton balls—and about who Janice believed she would turn out to be. I'm surprised she bothered to finish reading what I wrote. She wrote back: "Hi, All I can say is that I wish I could keep the orange girl as well as the red girl. She is very pretty and moves like a dream. All pups grow differently and she could turn out to be the largest. I only hope you don't have a problem getting her on the plane. They are not small. You will love her. Janice."

Somehow, that last sentence became not just an appraisal but a declaration. Yes, I would love her. Yes, there was something beyond tears and loss. There were endless fields and rises between death and here, and I was determined to take the trip again.

Two weeks later, I flew back to Baltimore on a Saturday morning, carrying only a shoulder bag and an empty soft Sherpa airline-approved puppy crate. Orange Girl had weighed eleven pounds at last report; I had purchased two tickets on AirTran—one human, one animal—so she could

46

ride in the cabin with me. Janice and Carol were driving the seventy miles to the Baltimore airport to meet me, and when I came into the main terminal, I saw them pushing a cart with a crate on top. I was twenty yards and a few seconds away from the baby talk that must be hardwired into the goo of maternal instinct. "Oh, muffin, you've gotten so big," I said to the puppy inside the crate, forgetting even to say hello to the humans accompanying her. They were smiling; these were people who were used to being ignored for their dogs. Janice opened the door to the crate and must have seen me hesitate: For a split second, I saw this: *brown eyes years of commitment terror white fur need love mine responsibility.* Janice said, with quiet certainty, "Take her." I gathered her into my arms, and at that moment Orange Girl became Tula, and we were on our way.

I had a two-hour delay before my flight back to Boston, and I spent it eating cheeseburgers with three Samoyed breeders, eavesdropping on show-dog talk. Janice and Carol and a fellow breeder were going to the Samoyed National in a couple of months, and they spoke in the impassioned code of conformation, structure and movement, championship points. Janice had convinced the air-terminal restaurant manager to seat us with a crate labeled LIVE ANIMAL, and so Tula sat just behind my shoulder, placid as a little monk.

• • •

Once we got to security, where we would separate, Janice's tough façade softened. She was giving up a pup she loved, and she pulled not one but five toys from her bag to ease the flight. I laughed at one alarming-looking bone she gave me and said, "I don't know if they'll let me on the plane with this." Ever the literalist, Janice shrugged and said, "Just tell them it's a knee." I hugged everyone, went through security with Tula in my arms. A security guy hollered down the line, "Hold up, there! Got to see the puppy." When I got to the waiting area for my flight, I found a couple of empty seats and sat down and unzipped the netted duffel bag, and a black nose emerged. I put my hand under the small, warm chin inside and talked to her, getting a lick and a nuzzle in return. Then I called the friend who was meeting my flight to tell her we were on time. "Kathy?" I said, and she heard the emotion there and said, "Are you all right?"

"Yes," I said, and my voice caught. Finally I said, "I feel like someone just put a poultice on my heart." We made plans to meet at the airport, said good-bye.

Then it was just us. No longer just me.

6.

....

Why do we love what we love? Is it an overlap of past and present, as Freud insisted, where the heart reaches for what is already gone? Or time and space colliding: We find nearby the object of our desire, whether the stray who shows up at the door or the stranger on a train. Biology may dictate most dramas of want, and age has plenty to do with it: Those goslings, loyal forever, reached out to Konrad Lorenz, the pioneer ethologist, because his was the first face and scent and touch they encountered. But did the need they displayed ensure his tenderness in return?

There's an old story, documented more than a decade ago, about a barren lioness in Kenya who adopted a series of oryx, or antelope, calves. The locals named the lioness Kamunyak, or "Blessed One." At first she toyed with the calf, unsure whether to protect it or make it her dinner. Then nurturance won out over predation, and the lioness mothered and defended the calf for months, until a male lion overpowered her and made off with the calf. Eventually Kamunyak began the same dance again, for weeks circling her territory alone, until she found another orphaned calf to bring into her fold.

I know this lioness; we all do. We are all a bit of her, blundering through life and finding purchase wherever the heart lands. It is a drama reenacted the world over and throughout time: hope against reality, carving out a few moments of magic and mutual comfort between the pure beginning and the equally certain end. We fix on attachment because we need it, as much as we need water and light and counting on tomorrow.

That lioness's supposed altruism was primal and selfish: If biology instructs that we care for our young as part of reproduction's dictates, we are also hardwired for nurturance. The payoff is in all those endorphins, oxytocin cascading through us from the moment we pick up an infant or a puppy or hear a baby coo. If we are lucky, we love what we love in part because the object is worth the effort. But sometimes the love itself—the elixir of desire—is enough to bestow the object with the transformative glitter it requires.

Being loved, I think, is another matter entirely, a neighboring city on the same train route, connected but by no means destiny. If and when the bond takes both ways, you have a third entity, which is the thing the lover and the loved create together. This is called history, or experience, and the stronger it is, the more power it has to muck about with the sense of self.

● ● ●

A lot of my adult life has been spent within shouting distance of others but in my own tent. Never married, no children, myriad levels of deep connection with men and women both. And animals: In my four decades of adult life, in three different cities, the longest time I ever spent without an animal was a little over a year. That was during my late twenties, when I was drinking too much; I had left an unhappy relationship, and left with it an extraordinary Persian cat named Rima. She heeled like a dog on walks around the park in Austin, Texas, killed a guinea hen once that was bigger than she, and selected my lap as a safe place to have a litter of kittens one night at 3 a.m. She had circled the room for hours until settling down in bed with me, then locked her eyes with mine during each yowling contraction. Every time Rima cried out, my own uterus heaved in reply, until she had four perfect kittens and then collapsed in sleep, inside the nest of me.

I had to get out of Texas, and I knew Rima was better off where she was, but for a long time I carried guilt and sorrow at having gone without her. I spent a year being drunk and scared on the East Coast before I found my way to another animal. Hoping to replicate history or maybe atone for my sin of abandonment, I got another silver Persian, this one a male, and brought him home to the attic garret in Boston where I had landed. He had huge, velvet-painting eyes and was afraid of everything except me, and for reasons I cannot fathom I named him Dashiell Hammett, maybe to give him courage or to add a sense of whisky-tinged bravado to the jam I was in. Dashiell lay on the pillows of my bed at night while I sat nearby, killing myself slowly with tumblers of Scotch. I loved him especially for this sentry duty, because he gave witness to my plight and kept me a few inches away from the cliff of being an existential washout. Whether I was drunk or hungover or caught in the limbo of craving, Dashiell was still and patient, my compass of responsibility; his litter box was always fresh and his pantry full, even when mine had more liquor bottles in it than anything else. I sometimes contended that I didn't love him much—he was timid and aloof and as petulant as Job—but when I had to put him down at the age of fifteen, I wailed as though someone had reached a fist into my chest.

But when Dashiell died, I had Clementine, who was by then a sassy young three-year-old, and I had Caroline, too, a singular best friend who shared with me our new, vast love for our dogs and for the soul-mate connection we shared. We counted on crossing the finish line together. For years when we talked about the future, we blanched at the idea of losing our dogs—a notion so grim that humor was our only defense. "Just think," Caroline liked to say. "When you're in your seventies, I'll be in my sixties, and we'll be staggering around Fresh Pond together. Lucille and Clementine will both be thirty-three."

We couldn't know that Caroline would be gone in just a few years, felled by cancer at forty-two. My world was so shaken by her death that I some-times felt I had to invent a whole new cast and script and stage direction. For the next six years Clementine flanked and protected me and gave me a reason to keep going. I had her until she was thirteen, and together we survived pit-bull attacks and human losses and the usual potholes and pathos of life, until she had to leave and I had to let her, and I suppose there are some things you never get over, don't even wish to.

One of the things you miss after someone dies is the shared fact of you. The we of me, I used to think of it, after Caroline was gone, and then Clemmie, too. The routine joys. The physical and emotional anchor: "This quiet dust / Was gentle-men and ladies. . . ."
We need to remember, I think, that dying isn't the worst thing. That getting to love someone on the way out is a great honor, easy to forget in the wake of so much sorrow.
For several years I went to Truro, on Cape Cod, in the summer and stayed in an eighteenth-

century house that bordered a riding stable. When I woke in the morning it was to the sound of horses whinnying and chuffing. A little goat named Blossom lived in the stable, too, to keep the horses company, though Blossom's temperament did not match her name. It was the horses whose sweetness enveloped the air like fresh grass.

One summer, I saw two teenage girls bury a horse they loved. The horse was old, and they had grown up riding him and had their first love affair with him, the way girls can do, horses being both safer and more dangerous than boys. It took a backhoe to bury the horse. A man brought in the backhoe and dug the hole, and then the large-animal veterinarian and the girls walked the horse down the hill, and the vet put him down there next to the giant hole. The girls cried as they braided flowers into his mane and placed pictures of them riding him in his grave. And two packages of potato chips, which he had loved.

Chris, Calliope, Kachina, Amoreena, Boofer, Eli, Rima, Lucky, Cory, Rex, Dashiell, Annie, Barley, Lucille, Cleo. Clementine. Shiloh. Tula. Those are some of the animals that have made my heart wider and wilder. All of them a one-way street to mercy, the totems through which we reach ourselves.

7.

....

Tula slept throughout the flight from Baltimore to Boston, her nose emerging only once to take a sip of water. I was so anxious, or so flooded with oxytocin, that I could barely stand to leave her in the airline's seat to walk to the bathroom five rows back—as though someone might try to steal her in a cabin at twenty thousand feet. When Kathy offered to hold her in the front seat of the car after she and her husband, Leo, had picked me up, I refused to relinquish her—and then worried, all the way home, that Leo was driving too fast. We drove up to my house just before dusk, and halfway down the block I realized there was a welcome sign out front: My twelve-year-old neighbor Sophie had hung a giant banner on my front porch that read WELCOME TO CAMBRIDGE, TULA!!!! I laughed in delight when I saw it, and then said to Kathy and Leo, "Oh, God—now everyone on the block will think I've adopted a little girl."

Kathy rolled her eyes. "Um, no," she said. "With you, they'll pretty much know it's a dog."

• • •

There's a school of thought that, upon losing a beloved animal, you should take care not to replace her too soon: In the midst of grief, no puppy can live up to the memories of the old dog, who had a lifetime to perfect her devotion. By these accounts, I probably came home with Tula too soon—three months after Clemmie died—but it seemed at the time the only tolerable and most pragmatic course of action.

Time is the sweet fog in which denial is wrapped. I had just seen Tula's sister from a previous litter, now two years old, springing like a fifty-pound bouncing ball at Janice's place. But I liked to believe I was ready for all of this. I had a fenced yard, the obligatory crates and baby gates, dozens of toys and training tools, years of experience. I had Shiloh, the four-year-old Belgian sheepdog down the street, and her owner, Peter, who had boundless energy and extraordinary instincts with animals. He and Shiloh had seen me through losing Clementine. "Be good to have a puppy around here," he said more than once that summer, upon walking into my too-quiet house. "Want Shiloh for a while?"

Now there was Tula: In the blink of an eye, it seemed, with simple letters and transactions and airplane flights, I had doubled the life force inside my house. For days after her arrival I reveled in this miracle. In the morning when I woke I heard her young breath, and then I opened my eyes and saw her looking at me from inside her crate by my bed, and I'd think, *My God, there's an animal in here,* and the day would begin. All puppies are a marvel when first encountering the world: They hiccup; their breath smells like sunshine; they chase their own shadows and the heart seizes in return. The adorability quotient in the very young —those big heads, those doelike eyes—is as vital to their survival as the food drive.

Introducing a Samoyed puppy to humans is a thing of easy beauty; they look like Gund teddy bears. Tula hung from my neck like a cub while I showed her around the neighborhood. Peter and his wife, Pat, came over to meet her the evening after we'd flown home. Peter's father had been a soldier in the Royal Horse Artillery in the British army, then a jockey and horse trainer, and Peter and his brothers had grown up working with horses and dogs in the stables. We had become friends through his first Belgian, Cleo, and I'd watched him for years with dogs—watched him deal with a skittish or fear-aggressive dog with one gesture. He was an architect by day and a lion tamer by instinct; if I asked him to explain why he'd done something, he often wasn't even conscious of it. That night he walked into the backyard with a huge smile on his face, sat down on the steps, picked up Tula, and put her inside his T-shirt. A white head popped out under his chin, hesitant but mostly delighted. In an instant he had done several crucial things, all of them with thoughtless affection. Tula now had his scent and his voice; she knew he was strong and in charge and had games to offer. In the months that followed, when she grew to fifty-five pounds and could haul a plow, I would think back on that first meeting with relief: Tula looked at Peter with adoration from that day on.

Perhaps she knew this was to be a lifetime position: For her first few days at home, Tula was a portrait of angelic calm. She accepted a leash and trotted next to me down the block, sitting quietly on my foot when she encountered anything new. She bunny-hopped through tall grass. She cocked her head at crickets. She talked to her toys, not with a bark but with a *woo-woo*. "You will love her," Janice had written, with declarative certainty. How hard could it be?

And then gradually, persistently, the charm had to make room for the young fiend who lurked within. After a few nights of routine Tula may have deduced that her new surrounds—the grassy backyard, the hovering human, the palace of chew toys—weren't going anywhere, and I watched as her careful reserve gave way to exuberance at the world around her. She was an exploding bottle of seltzer, most hours of every day. My small urban garden, beneath towering maples, had become an oasis of green in Clementine's last years; when I brought Tula home, at the end of summer, the yard was lined with stone pots of geraniums and tuberous begonias and border perennials. Two weeks later every flower on the property had been de-headed. Happy and animated by the sight of me, Tula hurled herself into me from any direction; I started calling her Sanorka's Attack from the Rear.

When she started teething she preferred me above all her chew toys, and for a month my forearms looked as though they'd been savaged by barracudas. I thought I knew all about teething puppies, and I tried every diversion possible: frozen washcloths, yelping in response, a shake can full of pennies. Tula seemed amused by my efforts. If I tried to pry her jaws off me, she would back up and bark in a wild frenzy. It was like having a baby fox in the kitchen. One night, during my allotted fifteen minutes of calm, when Tula was finally napping in her crate, I sat down at the computer to write Janice. My T-shirt and shorts were shredded; I had scabs up and down my arms. I had been brought down by a creature one-tenth my size. "Tula is really mouthy," I wrote Janice with bloodless calm. "Do you have any suggestions?"

"She must be getting her first teeth," replied

my pup's laconic breeder. "It's something they all go through. Give her some bones. Easily distractible." I dried my tears and walked back into battle.

I was banking on experience to get me through puppyhood, but much of that is academic before a dog reaches a certain age. What I really needed was staying power. Though I had the appetite of a warrior, I lost five pounds the first two weeks Tula was home; I was constantly stepping over baby gates, or carrying her outside, sometimes a dozen times a day. (She gained two pounds a week, which made her my own personal trainer.) After many hours of daily play, when Tula was settled in her crate, she looked at me with forlorn longing. Weren't there more holes to be dug, more arms and hands to be destroyed? I slept, when I slept, like a cinder block. After a few hours she'd whimper to go out, and I'd breast-stroke out of my REM sleep, gather her up, and head outside at 3 or 5 a.m. Some mornings I put her in her crate and pretended to leave the house, then went upstairs to sleep for another couple of hours.

Errands and exercise became my only retreat. "How are you?" a friend asked me one morning on the dock of the boathouse. "You look exhausted!"

"I have a new puppy," I said, and her face lit up.

Then I burst into tears. "I miss my old girl," I said, embarrassed and surprised by my display.

"Oh, but she's really young," said my rower friend, who had Portuguese water dogs and remembered. "She's still a baby!"

I was so sleep-deprived that I felt like an exposed nerve. I kept reminding myself that this was the fate of new motherhood, and that my body and energy levels were a couple of decades past that biological capability. One afternoon at the health club I went to sleep standing in the public shower a few yards from the pool, a semi-enclosed area where swimmers rinse off before and after swimming. I'd leaned against the wall and closed my eyes for a minute, and when I opened them again I realized I had stripped to the waist.

No doubt I half-dreamed that I was already in the locker room. I have no idea who had come and gone during my vertical nap, or how long it lasted. Struggling back into my wet suit, I imagined my response to a perplexed manager, alerted that there was a female flasher in the pool. "So sorry," I'd have to say. "New puppy. Won't happen again."

The rough moments were interspersed with awe while each little developmental miracle gave way to another. From the first days, when she responded to my recall whistle with only one repetition, I had recognized that Tula was smart and connected to the world around her, and I sensed there was a wonderful adult dog in my future. More immediately soothing was the sweet delight amid the frustration and fatigue: I'd see her chasing her shadow, or she'd go to sleep with her head on my shoulder, and I would melt in utter contentment. One morning the wind blew open a backyard door to the garage, and when I looked outside—I had left Tula alone for all of two minutes—she had gone in and selected three items: a swim buoy, a basket, and a push broom. She lined up the buoy and the basket, grabbed the broom handle in her teeth, and began pushing the items around in a circle like a tiny pony on an axle. It was an exclamation point of joy.

I have a note that I wrote to myself during those first few weeks of torment and happiness, in what seemed like an endless sea of physical and psychic demands. "I was worried I wouldn't love her," I wrote to myself, sometime in September, "and I love her so much I can't stand it. She is my little dancer and she is the candle in the cave."

8.

....

There's a note on my study wall, scribbled to myself one day and stuck there with a piece of tape. The note reads IT'S THE LIONESS, STUPID.

I kept this instruction for several reasons, the most obvious being to bring me back to the gist of my labors—raising my antelope calf, trying to find the reach from aloneness to connection. The note reminds me that the story is always about sacrifice, about Sisyphean effort, about failure and endurance and loving something more than and beyond yourself. Otherwise there would be no story at all.

The note reminds me, too, of my mother, whose sacrifices started long before those two hours on the living room floor with me each day. The oldest of six kids on a struggling Texas farm, she struck out for Abilene, a hundred miles away, when she was eighteen. It was the height of the Depression, and within a few years she had made it to Amarillo and put herself through business college, and was sending money home to her mother every month. By the end of the 1930s she owned her own car and a fur coat, and had enough bookkeeping and shorthand skills to be employable for the rest of her life.

I have a photograph of her taken from those years, around the time she met my dad. She is not yet thirty—a small, gorgeous brunette leaning on a telephone pole, her arms clasped coquettishly behind her. Her standing up against all that Texas Panhandle emptiness is enough to take my breath away.

For all the ordinary sorrows and failures of our struggling middle-class family, I think I always knew how much my parents loved each other. I had glimpsed the codes: an occasional locked bedroom door, a glance between them, the letters from my dad during the Second World War, which I found in the attic and surreptitiously read. I asked my mother politely one day—I was in my thirties, she past seventy—at what age people stopped making love. "I'll let you know," she said, and her eyes shined when she said it.

Maybe somewhere we know we are animals, with our musk and pheromones sending out mating calls to the nearby chosen. When my sister and I were young girls, my mother dressed up on special occasions to go out with my father. She usually wore the same black-chiffon-and-gold-lamé short evening dress, and she smelled like heaven. Pam and I would watch while she sat at her vanity doing her makeup, and sometimes she would get up and dance a few steps of the jitterbug or the Charleston or fox-trot to delight us. At the end of this grooming ritual, she dabbed perfume behind her ears, and then she and my dad disappeared into the night.

The perfume told me things I was otherwise too young to understand: that there was some milky language between beings, between my mom and dad, that was private and swoony. After I hit adolescence, I, too, loved perfume—Jungle Gardenia and Shalimar and all the heavy-sexy scents of Yardley Girl youth. The brands themselves were a tip-off: Tabu was gross; Prince Matchabelli was trashy. Patchouli oil soon became the über-aroma for wild girls from Austin to Berkeley, but then, in those early rock-'n'-roll days in Amarillo, the scent you wore told the rest of the tribe precisely who you were.

My mother's scent belonged to her alone. I can name every perfume it wasn't—Chanel, Joy, Estée Lauder. But I cannot locate what it was in my olfactory memory. Surely it would be a letdown, all that mystery confined to a brand name. It was the finishing touch of female perfection, dignified and off-limits, as enveloping as my father's love.

She never seemed to mind that I hadn't married. All those years of my riotous youth, she prayed that I would straighten up and fly right, in my father's words, and make a life that wouldn't disgrace the family. By the end of my twenties, after I had gone back to graduate school, she began to exhale a little. Then I moved to the Northeast in 1981, and the world that seemed so exotic to me became a thrilling place she loved to hear about and visit: trains to Manhattan, big-city newsrooms, the beaches of Cape Cod. Eventually, she came to feel that I had triumphed —first by becoming a writer, then by surviving my own demons.

My drinking, long an unspoken concern, went from two-fisted to frightening after I left Texas. Of this I told nothing to my mother. The narrative had split now: In her version, I was a freelance writer living in Boston, a "career girl," as she liked to say, independent and free. In the other story, the more complete one, I was consuming tumblers of Scotch or bourbon every night and writing in spite of this attachment. Then one terrible winter in 1984 I couldn't keep the half-truths separate anymore. I fell in a blackout and broke four ribs. I was thirty-three, and I look back now at that frightened young woman and see who my mother must have seen—someone who needed help and protection but couldn't accept either one. I spent another six months coming to terms with what sort of trouble I was in, then stopped drinking in July. And even though I went to hundreds of AA meetings and was a wreck for many months, I didn't tell my mother any of it until I thought I could bear the conversation.

For more than a decade I had made her crazy with worry, when I was hitchhiking cross-country or protesting the war and wearing my defiance like a shield. But now that I was sober, I knew that my drinking had been as dangerous as the other risks I had taken. Alcohol and depression had claimed victims on both sides of my family, and probably because I was so scared myself, I didn't want my mother to know how bad it was at the end: an attic apartment full of whisky bottles and despair and scribbled notes I wrote to myself during blackouts.

I told her a softer account when I went home to Amarillo that Christmas, six months after I had stopped drinking. She was quiet when I told her, and we didn't talk much about it for the rest of the trip. About two months later she called me in Boston for our weekly conversation, and said she had something to tell me: that she, a social drinker for years, had stopped drinking soon after I left and hadn't taken a drink since. I can still hear her explaining why. "I figured if my daughter could do something that she said was the hardest thing she'd ever done in her life," she told me, "then I could do it with her."

The kindness of this act stops me now, nearly

three decades later, with the purity of its intent. My mother lived a day's plane ride away, and her giving up alcohol would have no discernible consequence in my life. I know now that she was doing it not just for the support it engendered but for the intimacy it foretold: Whatever hell I had been through and was still struggling with, she wanted to get in there with me. Down on the floor again: Here, honey, I'll do them with you.

She went to a couple of Cambridge AA meetings with me over the next few years. "My name is Ruby," she invariably said, "and I'm visiting from out of town."

"Hi, Ruby!"

She was eighty-three the last time she came, wearing a hot-pink tracksuit, and I watched her charm everyone in the room. We drove to Provincetown the next day, and while we were shopping she bonded greatly with a gay storekeeper; he mistook my mother for my older girlfriend, and kept referring to her as my companion. I knew she would be flattered by this error and so told her when we left the store. For weeks after she returned to Bible Belt Texas, she signed every letter she wrote to me, "Your companion."

When I had been sober about five years, I fell in love with a man my mother might have imagined in a fairy-tale ending: He was soft-spoken and brilliant, a decade older, with an Ivy League pedigree to go along with his accomplishments and charm. Because she was a farmer's daughter who had gauged progress as the distance between Abilene and Amarillo, I privately feared that she would be too easily dazzled by this romance. The real story was less glamorous and more conflicted. I had fallen hard for a man with a tangled past and outsized ego, and even though I had stopped drinking and was in the middle of building a good life on my own, I lost my footing with him.

I was mind-numbingly attached to him, so that his disappearance was the one thing I could not tolerate, and he wielded this weapon with strategic acumen. Most of our two-year romance was a narrative out of O'Neill that holds allure, I think, only up to a certain age. Our passions were dramatic and insane: He hung up on me long distance, for no reason and with no warning; he broke a dinner date on my birthday at 6 p.m. We declared undying love for each other and a week later decided we needed a sabbatical—we split up the weeks for a summer rental we had taken in Wellfleet, and when I came home from work that night, he had moved all his clothes out of my apartment. By the end of three weeks of radio silence, I had lost seven pounds and was sitting on my upstairs porch in the middle of the night, smoking Winstons and staring into space.

More than two decades later, I am in my office overlooking the tree-lined street where I've lived—with dogs, no humans—for eleven years. A house of my own, a room somewhere with an enormous chair. Was I ever that young woman, wild-eyed with want, skinny and strung out and with my heart on a sacrificial slab? Of course I was: The picture is a cliché of female desperation. Maybe love always contains this potential toxin, unleashed when power eclipses self-regard. But I could claim neither one, not then on the porch at 3 a.m., and not when my mother called every few days to check in. For her sake I put a good face on it, and told her I was OK and not to worry. One day she interrupted me and said abruptly, "Honey, don't take a drink over this man. No man on earth is worth your picking up a drink."

My heart exhales when I remember her voice saying those words—that piercing message, delivered like an arrow to the unconscious. I hadn't known I was close to a drink, but she did, and she knew it would be the worst thing and that she might be able to stop it. And she did—she stopped my free fall. The ledge of my mother, as I dropped through space. I hung up the phone that day and went to my first Al-Anon meeting, a great way station for emotional entanglements, and by the time Henry Higgins came back from his sabbatical I had taken hold of the ground again.

A few months later Ruby came to visit. The psycho-love was still going on, though within the year it would die a comet's death, and I would be more relieved than anguished. But that summer I was still wanting things to work out, still wanting everything to be better and different, and we had planned a dinner for Mom to meet S. She had brought the finest thing in her closet for the occasion, a beautiful Chanel suit that my sister had given her. By early afternoon the day of the dinner, S. still hadn't checked in. I hadn't talked to him in two days and was trying to hide my panic. (He had a history of fleeing crucial moments.) Ruby and I were standing at my closet, looking over her clothes and mine, and I sighed and said, as calmly as possible, "I hope tonight works out."

My mother straightened herself up and said, "Now listen, honey. Either I'll wear this suit tonight, or I'll wear it to his funeral."

We had dinner that night as promised, and S. was the one who was dazzled: my stylish West Texas mother, who was both humble and proud and afraid of no man. When I look back on that period of my life—the marathon thirties, when I got sober, fell in and out of love a couple of times, found work that I loved—my mother is a hovering presence throughout my inner land-scape, even though I got to see her only about once a year. And I think it was then, when I was alone in a new city and finding my way, that I realized how strong she was, how utterly fearless when it came to protecting her cub. My father was the John Wayne patriarch who had scared half the boys in Amarillo during his daughters' adolescence, and because his presence was so large and blustery and beloved, he had always seemed like the gatekeeper to my safety. But when I grew up and hit the four-lane highway of adulthood—when I was drunk and two thousand miles away, or falling apart over some man—it turned out to be Ruby who had my back.

9.

....

The most dramatic decisions I've made in my life feel now as though they were launched by a level-headed unconscious: leaving Texas, stopping drinking, getting clear of bad relationships. Occasional leaps of faith toward the unknown that seemed cockeyed or frightening but turned out well. This sort of broad jump was behind my getting Tula when I did. As much as I wanted a puppy before another winter took its toll, I think there was a more urgent imperative at work—some inner counsel saying, *Do this now—we are working with a deadline here.*

By late autumn Tula had grown from eleven to thirty-five pounds, and had the stature and attitude of a small white wolf. I could still carry her around at that weight, and I have a photo of the two of us, with me looking skeptical but proud. She is poised on my shoulder with a queenly gaze that makes me laugh to remember it. The confidence that Janice and Carol had glimpsed in a seven-week-old puppy—"She pulls herself up," Carol had written about her show-dog posture—asserted itself in adolescence with an imperious presence that was by turns lovely and horrifying. Tula expected the world to be a wonderful place, there to delight her. Occasion-ally she noticed that I had something to do with the way the day unfolded—its walks and car rides and tennis balls—but more often I was treated as an affable sidekick, or valet; like most sled dogs, she seemed to assume that her job was to lead and mine to follow.

This is not a negotiation resolved quickly or simply. It takes a combination of brute strength, conviction, and good cheer to persuade Samoyeds that you are more important than their destination. They respond to praise and laughter, but if you bully them, they will simply sit down, look away, and refuse to move. If you lose patience at this point in the game, you will regret it. And if you yell at them or show anger, they will forgive you for being an idiot, but they will have made note.

Walking in the woods one day, I met an elderly Russian man and his wife who smiled in delight over Tula, revealing their familiarity with the breed with the Russian pronunciation ("Ah! Sam-o-YED!!!"). They told me, in faltering English, about their experience with the dogs back in Russia. "Good dogs!" the man told me, smiling. "But they are not listening!" Indeed, sir, they are not listening, a present-tense state of mind that can seem as though it will go on forever.

●●●

Tula came into her physical strength during one of the worst winters in recent history: ice and snow and relentless cold, all of which thrilled her and disheartened me. I had been teaching her to heel since the first few weeks she was home, and one afternoon when she was about nine months old, during a leash walk around the neighborhood, she lunged at the sight of a squirrel and almost took me down. I popped her collar and told her to settle; when I got no response I raised my voice and told her to sit. She turned and looked at me, and then raised up on her hind legs like a bear—a stance of all bluff that amuses me now but infuriated me at the time. It was the end of winter and I was exhausted; Tula's energy and bearing had by now convinced me that I had a strong-minded dog who would prove a challenge to the ablest thirty-year-old. And so I yelled at her, standing there on the street in my Cambridge neighborhood, surrounded by houses with neighbors who knew us both. "I am going to win this battle!" I hollered, and Tula cocked her head, perplexed at the new words and new tone in my voice. Then she abandoned her fixation on the squirrel and trotted home next to me, undeterred and self-assured, no more interested in my moment of street rage than she was in yesterday's dinner.

• • •

While I have been remembering these early combat zones, Tula has gone to sleep on the brick patio in my backyard, a couple of yards away from me, with a fleecy blue sheep in her mouth. Before she drifted off, she was making little nibbling gestures on the toy, an oral comfort she has engaged in from puppyhood. It is a simulation of nursing at the mother's teat, and I used to let her do this on my watchband or my T-shirt, so that she would tie that suckling instinct to me—so that she would let me be the lioness who adopted her. In return I vowed not to maul her, or make her my dinner. Maternal self-sacrifice is what keeps us from eating our young.

She has grown into a magnificent, confident creature so aware that she can sense my every move and the tone in my voice from three rooms away. We love what we love in spite of ourselves, toward something larger and more generous than the velvet prison of self.

Years ago, I met a woman who loved to photograph her beautiful daughter. She told me once, half-laughing, that she enjoyed looking at the photos more than raising the girl. The girl started stealing at sixteen, looking for love in all the wrong places. Maybe this is the narcissist's lament, or maybe it's just human: You love your daughter more on prom night than on the morning she announces she hates you.

Will Tula start to steal? What's the canine equivalent of acting out? I think we're all right on that score; she knows thoroughly that she is loved. Dogs are the mirrors of our humanity. That's one reason they get kicked around: They are such loyal witnesses, and bad people can't stand to be seen.

So I will choose the living, the choice we must keep on making. I will choose my living, imperfect, bossy dog over the glistening scrim of memories I have bestowed upon the past. We need imperfection in our relationships, else we would die from the thickness of intimacy. We probably need the I-hate-yous, the spit-up on the baby blanket, to be able to bear how much we love them.

I do wish I could leave a few notes for the dead, to give them crucial details. To tell my mother that I am all right: strong and safe and still planting the field pansies and red geraniums she loved at the start of every spring. I would like my dad to know that his memory still causes a physical sensation of warmth in my heart, like being held from the inside out. I wish I could wrap my arms around Clementine, and tell her she's my good girl always.

And I wish Caroline knew how much my loving her, even after her death, has made me a better friend in the world. She would like that, I think.

10.

....

"This is a rotten dog!" Tula was trespassing in the bunny patch at Fresh Pond Reservoir again, and Ranger Jean was having a meltdown. For the past ten minutes I had been trying to coax Tula out of her Elysian fields, an off-limits marsh of grasses that held field mice and the occasional brown rabbit. When Jean drove by in her orange mini-truck, I was sitting on the hill gazing at the meadow, hoping that the park ranger might overlook a fifty-pound white dog pouncing at the ground in delight.

Jean killed the engine, arranged her state trooper–like hat, and crossed her arms. "Looks like there's a sheep on the loose," she announced, and started down the hill.

"White dog," she hollered—futilely, given that Tula didn't know she was a white dog—"get over here!" Tula pranced away. The worst thing you can do to catch a wayward dog, particularly a mischievous one, is to run toward it yelling. The dog was no fool: Why approach an angry stranger in a big hat?

When Jean turned to me and declared, from

twenty yards away, what a rotten dog Tula was, my heart sank and I yelled back. "Don't say that," I shouted. "It isn't helping." I plunged into the marsh and slipped on a patch of grass; only then, when Tula saw me go down, did she run my way. I grabbed hold of her foot-long training lead and we headed up the hill to face our accuser.

After I'd wriggled away from Jean's lecture, I walked around, brooding. For months I had been immersed in the territory of off-lead training, using Shiloh the Belgian sheepdog as a role model, doling out chicken and exuberant praise. But Tula was proving enough of a huntress to require wide parameters to keep her safe. When her nose got the better of her, she ignored my commands with happy abandon. I liked to say it was easy to train a Samoyed as long as you had the right tools: in one pocket a bag of freeze-dried liver for the dog, in the other, a handful of Xanax for the human.

Today Shiloh had waited nearby during Tula's happy romp, then sat next to me while Jean and I talked, her sheepdog focus as fixed as that of a member of the K-9 Corps. I made a final loop of the peninsula with the dogs and stopped to rest. My cell phone interrupted my sad reverie; I knew it would be Peter, calling to check in.

"How's it going?" he asked.

"I'm exhausted," I said. "Tula went in the

bunny patch and we got busted. Ranger Jean called her a rotten dog. My leg is starting to hurt. I think I'm losing my mind."

"Wow," said Peter, already half-listening, even though he liked my dispatches from the front. "Sounds like a lot of drama."

"Oh, you know me," I said. "Every day is a little bit of *King Lear.*"

The external picture of those first two years with Tula must have been a far cry from my experience of the story. I remember being tired and grumpy all the time; in photos, I look ridiculously happy. My neighbor Nancy, who adored Tula and believed her incapable of bad behavior, used to cover her ears and sing whenever I would complain. And yet my dog's intelligence outweighed even my worst frustrations; I was banking on it to keep her interested as well as to keep her safe.

I began exploring woods in every direction outside of Cambridge, places vast and remote where Tula could run and I could train her off-lead without having a heart attack. She looked like a white wolf running through the woods, her nose and eyes giving her information I could only guess at. I knew that to call her in to me during the height of her excitement was futile, and could also be perceived as confining, so I began giving her instruction from afar. I walked a forest path while she ran in the hills and rises above it, and when she ran parallel to the path and looked my way, I praised her—"Watch me, good dog!"— without asking her to come in. I tried to give her enough rein to have her *want* to come back to me: an exacting formula that is different with every dog.

One afternoon, toward the end of a long walk, when Tula was chasing squirrels on a steep hill, I started up in her direction, only to realize the incline was too difficult for me to scale. I grabbed a long stick and half-dragged myself up, wondering, as usual, what had possessed me to think I was a match for this animal. Two different breeders over the years had picked puppies for me they described as "very spunky." Very spunky is cute at eleven pounds, less so at fifty. I had been flattered by those breeders' assumptions, and I was suffering the consequences of my vanity. By the time I got to the top of the hill, I was out of breath and cursing, my heart pounding and my weak leg crying out in protest. Tula was waiting nearby, wagging her tail at my appearance and standing near an older woman who regularly walked there with her Labrador retriever. When she saw me scramble up the last few feet with my tree branch, the woman called out to me. "Good God!" she boomed. "You look as though you're about to lance a boar!"

•••

This somber appraisal, delivered in an old Yankee diction, was funny enough to penetrate my vault of self-pity. I spent the rest of the walk contemplating the dissonance between her perception and my reality, her observation that I was charging forward with my staff while I felt I was staggering through space.

The truth was that too many days lately I was limping instead of ambling. But I also knew that Tula's adolescence was finite, and that my endurance race had an end in sight. If I could just maintain my strength for the next year or so, both of us—me and this indomitable creature I had chosen to love—were going to be fine. "Three years," a trainer had told me, "and you'll have a soul mate." So far, that seemed about right.

I had several dreams during this time that were the usual mumble of the unconscious under stress. Most of them were obvious, like the one where I was walking the neighborhood at 3 a.m. with a lion on a rope. But one morning I woke from a deep sleep trying to remember some absurd script I had been lost in. In the dream, Tula had been lying in a relaxed position, her front paws splayed outward, a familiar stance in real life that I referred to as seal yoga. Two men I didn't know—I assumed they were physicians—came over and spoke to me with a sense of concern.

"You're handling this really well," one of the men in the dream told me, and though at first I was confused, it became clear as he spoke that Tula had a degenerative muscular condition similar to ALS. What I had thought of as an endearing pose was in fact something terrible and progressive, a disease the doctors referred to as "brace."

I woke up with a start of fear and then relief, reassured by the sound of a healthy dog breathing a few feet away, and by the time I was fully awake I'd forgotten it. Until hours later, when I was walking the pond, and the dream came back to me. I thought about the oddness of the word *brace*—was it a brace of dogs, or a verb for the resolute nature of my task? My thickheadedness is testament to how thoroughly an old fear of mine had been repressed. It took another day for me to make the connection, and when I did I was driving, and I pulled over to the side of the road to write these notes to myself:

> brace. the name of the condition Tula had. killing slowly realizing seal yoga was inability to move. just realized 4 pm that brave [*sic*] is POLIO.

Here's the translation of that roadside short-hand: "Brace" was from one of the worst memories of my childhood, when our orthopedic

83

surgeon advised my mother to make me wear a metal leg brace at night, with the goal of stretching my Achilles tendon. I think I was about five. She told me years later that she woke in the middleof the night to hear me screaming. I remember disconnected shards of the experience: the cold-ness of the metal, the searing pain that woke me, the territory between fear and helplessness that must be particular to a child's experience. And I remember the sound of her running down the hall, which has eclipsed the misery of the night itself.

The notion that I had planted this old memory onto my innocent young dog told me two things. One was how much I loved and wanted to protect her, in spite of the day-to-day frustration I felt about her antics. The second lesson was deeper, more obscure, and it took longer to figure out. It was this: that I had been tripping along through life in every sense, downplaying by light of day what had happened to me half a century earlier. But I was still frightened, at least on some dark, unspoken level. I suspect I had known for a while that the past not only wasn't past, but that it might be getting worse.

11.

··

Boar-lancing fantasies aside, I was plagued by self-doubt during a lot of Tula's young life, and only later did I see how much my sense of inadequacy had a physical base. Strength in a powerful dog is different from defiance, though I often mistook one for the other—when Tula wanted to go forth with an athlete's exuberance, and I misread her eagerness as some insouciant wildness that I couldn't tame. I knew I could outfox her, and probably outlast her ("I am going to win this battle!"). But much of training requires an agility I was realizing that I no longer had. Teaching a dog to heel means walking at different speeds and making quick U-turns; teaching a big dog not to jump on people is most effectively accomplished by grabbing her paws and dancing, or by planting a knee in the dog's chest. My chief advantage, besides patience, was an obsessive nature: I didn't mind the endless repetition that training demands. I'd been teaching her commands of restraint since she was a puppy: "gentle," for taking food or a ball from me, and "careful," for slowing it down. If I took a pratfall in the woods or outside, she ran up to me and began licking my face—a sign of connection as well as concern.

I had been falling a lot lately, and spending energy trying not to notice. Denial had long been part of my m.o. in fighting the aftereffects of polio, and sometimes it served me well, especially when it came to compensating for what my leg couldn't do. I had good upper-body strength, and until recently I'd been able to rely on a makeshift balancing act to get around. But in the past couple of years, I had begun to lose my footing in ways that were annoying, then distressing. This had less to do with handling Tula, I had to admit, than with my own unsteadiness—or clumsiness, as I thought of it on the bad days. I didn't just fall on ice; I fell on a clear sidewalk. I tripped; I stumbled; I lurched. And I always had a quick recovery at the ready, for myself and for everybody else.

My limp was more pronounced when I was tired, more noticeable when someone viewed me from the front, walking toward them. Sometimes people I had known casually for years would ask why I was limping. My answer was standard, and went along these lines: "You know I limp a little, remember?" Or, "Oh, my leg's sore; it's just from rowing." When strangers asked, I had an automatic answer that was quick and vague: "I have a bum leg; I'm fine."

But the questions were coming, I had to concede, with alarming frequency—and from friends and strangers alike: *Why are you limping? What did you do to your leg? Ow, that looks like it hurts!* With strangers, the affect ranged from genuine concern to an odd form of rubber-necking, the latter of which had finally begun to get on my nerves. Physical infirmities are a Rorschach for all kinds of emotional responses, from fear to compassion. What got to me were the curious people who pressed for an answer, then seemed embarrassed if I said I'd had polio—as though it were cholera, and possibly contagious, or as if I'd just gotten out of prison. I'd learned to deflect the careless inquiries and embrace the nice guys, who were in the majority. One of the first things I had liked about Peter was the way he addressed this part of me within weeks of our meeting, sometime in 2002. We were walking the dogs down the block to our neighborhood park, and he asked matter-of-factly, "Why do you limp?" When I told him he said, "Wow! You had *polio?*" As though it were an adventure, or special circumstance, which I suppose in some ways it was.

A version of this, though, is always going on from the moment two people's time and space collide: Subtle or direct, we are negotiating the private and public spheres. If the wounds are on the inside, we have some choice about what to reveal when, and to whom. If the scar is on the outside—the physical signature that announces itself with the nuance of a trumpet—people tend to think they know a great deal about you, whether they do or not.

I usually made intuitive choices about when to mention polio, but my one rule was not to mention it to coaches—not until I needed to—because I didn't want to be pitied or mollycoddled. I didn't want them to discourage me or assume I was the half-capable one they had to train. This strategy worked for years, but my clear decline on land was making it harder to pull off.

What fears I had I did not share. I knew about the cluster of symptoms referred to as post-polio syndrome, or PPS, and I vacillated between trying to educate myself about it and acting as though it didn't exist. Sometimes late at night I would go to the National Institutes of Health website, and read and reread the official statement there on the condition. I read it furtively, as though I were taking the Twenty Questions drinking quiz, and sometimes my stomach would sink while I was reading, and the next day I pretended I hadn't read it at all.

The syndrome occurs more often and more savagely with those whose original case of polio was severe, and can result in further muscle loss and incapacitating fatigue. The first person I knew who had suffered from PPS was the mother of an old boyfriend; she had had polio as a young girl, recovered well enough to walk with a cane as an adult, but was in a wheelchair by fifty. A trip to a neurologist when I was forty had eased my distress about the phenomenon, because, he told me, the more neurons lost, the less you have to work with; normal aging takes away muscle mass, so the effects are more extreme in an already compromised body. In other words, the greater the damage done at the onset of the disease, the greater the potential for fallout in later years. Evidence suggested I would be all right: I had learned to row in middle age, and was hell-bent on being one of the exceptions. A Pilates instructor had asked me in my early fifties if I was worried about using up my exercise capacity—she had known polio survivors who did only very light workouts, afraid they were exercising against the hourglass.

All these were anecdotal insights, empirically useless for my condition, whatever it was. I tried for years to block the entire notion of post-polio syndrome from my daytime consciousness. I was already doing everything prescribed: moderate exercise, plenty of sleep. And so denial seemed the best course of action, given the NIH-stated prognosis: no treatment, no cure.

12.

The falling was one thing, but pain was another country entirely. And for the first time that I could remember, beyond the normal sprains and injuries associated with falling, I was experiencing it on a regular basis. This had sneaked up on me, in the way that most cataclysms reveal themselves first as hairline cracks. I had calf cramps and muscle aches and groin strains, my leg got cold at night, no matter how many blankets I covered it with, and sometimes it would simply buckle, as though protesting all the work demanded of it.

I had ways of explaining each of these, ways of convincing myself that each twinge or ache or spasm was transient, understandable. It was when I started comparing myself with the person I'd been a few years earlier that the picture grew somber. In the not-so-distant past I had felt impervious to the most energetic dogs; now I held on to the fence at Fresh Pond whenever a big dog came up to greet me. The three-mile circuit from my house around the reservoir, once manageable, seemed herculean. When I did it at all, it took me a couple of hours. Tula's energy level charted some of this decline for me. Walking with Peter or Nancy, she heeled like a model obedience dog, but she always lunged ahead with me. After she had learned the pace of normal walkers, she couldn't comprehend why I moved so slowly by comparison.

That autumn, in 2009, I went to visit friends in Austin who saw me every few years. Three different people expressed alarm at how pronounced my limp had become, even when I reminded them that I had had polio and was simply getting old like everyone else. At the insistence of a friend who had known me for decades, I made an appointment with an orthopedic surgeon as soon as I returned home. He had been around during the pioneering rehab on polio patients in the 1950s, and he could tell at a glance, even through my baggy cargo pants, which muscles had been affected and how.

I told him about the falls I had taken in the past two years—I'd counted thirteen, though there may have been more. Still, he was philosophical, encouraging. He suggested balance exercises and gave me a prescription for physical therapy. He told me he still downhill-skied. He shrugged when I mentioned pain. "You're like every polio patient I've ever met," he told me. "You have a can-do attitude." I didn't want to disappoint him with my grim list of questions, but I plowed ahead. "What about post-polio syndrome?" I asked him. "I've been doing a lot of reading about it."

He smiled. "And what," he asked me, "does Wikipedia have to say about PPS?"

I swallowed the insult and said that my research was from a renowned rehabilitation hospital and the National Institutes of Health official statement on the syndrome. Then he explained why he believed it was a vastly exaggerated or alarmist interpretation of normal aging, enhanced by polio's early (but finite, or self-limiting) effects. It was comforting to share this doctor's optimism about me: He cheered on my lifestyle (big dog, swimming, rowing) and he seemed to view me as a glass-half-full type whose pain was negligible but whose spirit was not. I felt elated when I left his office—*I can get stronger! Post-polio syndrome doesn't exist!*—and tried, for the next several months, to live up to his image of me. I went home and ordered the walking stick he had suggested, then parked it in the closet.

After navigating ice all that winter, I stumbled in the backyard the next spring and landed hard on a flagstone, fracturing my left forearm. The break took a while to diagnose. I called my primary-care doctor and went in for an X-ray: A physician's assistant didn't touch my arm but sent me straight to radiology, ordering views of my elbow, not my radius. Two weeks later, when the pain became sharper after I lifted heavy pots in the garden, I went back for more X-rays. The doctor called that night and left a message. "The bad news is that your arm is broken," she said. "The good news is that it seems to be healing well without us!" I vowed, not for the first time, to change practitioners.

A few weeks later I came home on the train from New York, spending most of the nearly four-hour ride with my legs stretched out in front of me. When we arrived at Back Bay Station in Boston and I tried to stand, a shooting pain went down the side of my leg that was so debilitating I was afraid I couldn't walk. I made it out of the station in three efforts, stopping and sitting on my rolling suitcase, then walking another twenty or so yards. By the time I got to a cab I was sweating, probably from the adrenaline it took to get me there.

My doctor diagnosed severe sciatica, and gave me a referral to physical therapy.

Danielle was a young, willowy woman who was pleasant but all business. Twice a week, I showed up at her office to do leg lifts and core strengtheners and planks and cobras, then went home with a series of resistance bands and exercises I vowed to do daily. Usually I did them on the night before my next appointment, so that

I could pretend I'd been keeping to schedule.

Maybe my reluctance was typical—it's hard to do prescribed floor exercises when you're tired and in pain and no one's watching. But I think I had an extra dose of defeat tied to any effort to strengthen my leg. When I got on the floor, Tula usually brought me a tennis ball mid-routine, so I got the comic relief I needed, and we would play a round of nose billiards before I began again. Inevitably, though, I felt the familiar impotence of that cold floor in Amarillo. Partly it was the pain this time around; maybe some of it was aging, which seemed these days to carry a mood of cauterized hope. But it felt like a darker, more specific knowledge of some downhill course I was on. The lightest excursions were tiring to think about. Dinner with a friend—well, I don't know; how far a walk is the restaurant from the car? Meet Peter at the park for a ten-minute dog walk, a half-block away? Sorry, not tonight. If I forgot something in a far aisle of the grocery store, I'd do without. Even in my beloved woods I took shortcuts on the path to save ten steps. Rowing was only a little kinder. I could still get in a few miles, but it took me the rest of the day to recover. The only place where I felt free of pain, unafraid of falling, was in the water.

I realize this now; I did not know it then. Chronic pain is a mean strategist—it takes away your life a little at a time. Acknowledging it goes against some primitive instinct of survival, and so one adapts by denying. This applies to all kinds of trouble: We find ways to anesthetize ourselves to bad situations. It's easier, at least in the beginning, to pretend the antagonist isn't there—or will go away, or not do it again, or not turn out to be such a problem after all. It's always easier to wait until tomorrow to make the call. Then you look up and the trouble has bullied you into a corner of the room and eclipsed everything else in your life.

I began to grasp what was happening to me only by watching the rest of the world. I marveled when I saw people older than I who were striding through airports, or jogging the pond, or moving with a security I hadn't experienced in ages. I was traveling that summer, and I usually had a few good hours in the day if I timed it right and could stretch out in a pool. But I sagged in relief when I got to a hotel room at the end of the night, where I could count on room service and pain-killers to buy me some relief.

I saw Danielle throughout the fall. One morning, at her office, I decided to come clean. I was lying on the table and doing side leg lifts, which I loathed because they told me how weak my right leg had become. When I finished the set I turned to her and said, haltingly, "I have a confession to make—I haven't really been sticking with the program. I've been feeling pretty defeated."

I was counting on a sympathetic response, some magic bullet of encouragement or optimism. Instead I saw a grim, slightly impatient look on Danielle's face. She straightened up from the foot of the table and crossed her arms.

"Well," she said, "it's not up to me to motivate you—I get paid whether you're here or not. And I can't promise you that if you do these exercises religiously, they'll work. The only thing I can guarantee is that if you don't do them, you won't get any better."

I went home to get Tula and headed for the woods. We spent the afternoon walking the trails in autumn light, with Tula ranging after chipmunks and me feeling the sting of Danielle's ice-water pronouncement. On one level I recognized its truth: It was not up to her, a half-stranger, to move me to change my body or my life. And I knew her attitude was not my problem, that she had been cold and unforgiving, and was in no position to judge me. But knowing those things had no effect on how leveled I felt by what she had said. I was flooded with a sense of failure, of what I now know was shame, and the dissonance of this emotion was a marker for me. Only the past can cast such a deep shadow on the present. What I was feeling that day was something I had felt as a girl, and I'd spent most of my life trying never to feel it again.

"Well, you know, Mom really drop-kicked us out of childhood," my sister is saying, during one of our endless conversations about our complementary but different versions of the past. As the more well-behaved older sister, Pam finished college, moved to Dallas, got a job. Like most young adults on the verge of mammoth responsibility, she may not have been ready to be drop-kicked; I was so long-gone already that I hardly noticed. Part of my footloose confusion was encouraged by the cultural rebellion around me, which, by 1973, had sent me from Austin to San Francisco and Berkeley, then to Taos, New Mexico, and back to Austin. I could barely remember to notify my parents what city I was in. But history always shows up to interpret our personal imprints, to corral them into some larger social truth. I suspect my rebellions, often unspoken but bone-deep, would have surfaced no matter what the circumstances.

Was this the beginning of a tough persona, one that carried me many miles and years but ultimately had to be dismantled? Toughness can sometimes get you out of a rough spot on a dark street, but it can also get you killed, and it's not all that useful when you're facing private demons at 3 a.m. Toughness helped to get me out of

Texas, and might have pushed me into news-rooms, fueled by adrenaline and testosterone. I'm less sure that it got me, say, to my first AA meeting, or into a therapist's office, or into the muck of vulnerability that every love affair is. All these I had encountered, and at some point toughness becomes just another cliché, a veneer that has fooled somebody, for better or worse.

I had an editor for many years who was smart and stubborn, who drove his writers with equal parts praise and tyranny. We were fond of each other, and sneaked away from the newsroom more than once to go to a Red Sox game. Like my dad, he believed me incapable of failure, or at least any admission of failure. He asked me one day why I was limping—he had known me at least five years—and I said, "You remember; I had polio. I always limp."

"Oh," he said. "I always thought that was a swagger."

Tough is different from strong, of course, and sometimes it's easy to be strong: hospital corridors, gravesides, emergencies. The hardest times are when no one is watching, and it doesn't really matter whether you're strong or not. The times when you think life is circling the drain, and the bedrock aloneness of it trumps everything else. That's when animal instinct kicks in, and most of us start to crawl toward the light. Every soldier knows this, and probably every mammal. We like to call it courage, but the body doesn't recognize it as such. You just put your head down and keep moving.

13.

....

By the end of that week, my sense of defeat over Danielle's dismissal had turned into something else. I started walking farther at the reservoir. I'd barely closed out the rowing season that year, reaching my minimum required mileage from the boathouse where I was a member, and by December I had lengthened my walk in the woods to the reservoir's entire circumference, about two miles. I didn't mind that it took me nearly two hours. The dogs—I usually had both Tula and Shiloh—were accustomed to my amble, and they ran the hills above me as I walked. The pain I felt on city streets was softened by walking on pine-forest floor, and every time I made it all the way around the reservoir was a promise that I might do it again, might beat back the pain with muscle-building.

Then winter hit, snowstorms and ice that didn't melt until the following April. I often met my friend Jean and her cockapoo, Max, for walks, and some days I had to hang on to her as well as to the fence. We wore crampons for the ice and I started picking up a fallen branch at the beginning of every walk to use as a staff. When the ice melted, I kept using it. The pool at the end of the day offered its usual relief. But I tried stretching and resting, tried walking and not walking, and no matter what I did I felt a pain so thorough and migratory I could barely explain or isolate it.

I told almost no one about the pain, about how ever-present it was, and I didn't voice my worst-case scenario: that this was polio's legacy, and would end in a wheelchair. Tula ran to me whenever I fell, but what filled me with despair was her adapting to what was now routine. Accustomed to my groans when I sat down inside the house, she still looked my way, but no longer with any surprise. The noise had become as familiar as car keys or laughter.

In early March I went to see a new primary-care physician—a man who had long cared for a friend and who came highly recommended. After the mishaps and half-measures of the past couple of years, all I really hoped for was a sympathetic ear and a meeting about coping with chronic pain. Dr. Ranere was a big, friendly man who seemed immediately engaged: with me, my medical history, medicine itself. I delivered the usual sketch—polio as an infant, years of exercise and strengthening, recent years of pain. When he asked me where it hurt, my brain was so overloaded with information that I became confused. Had no one ever asked me where it hurt before? I can't remember. I know only that I started with the lower part of the leg and worked up, using my hand as a guide, and said, "Here, and here, and here, and here . . ."

Within twenty minutes, Dr. Ranere had been more thorough and thoughtful than anyone I'd seen in the medical profession in years. He considered a visit to a neurologist to ascertain the residuals of polio, but told me he was puzzled by my symptoms. "Polio is a neurological disease," he said. "It explains the weakness but not the pain. What did the MRI show?"

There had been no MRI, ever, and I told him so.

"OK, what about the X-ray?" Same answer. In the twenty or so years I had been experiencing difficulty—sprains and injuries and progressive weakness and discomfort—no one, in ortho-pedics or internal medicine or neurology or physical therapy, had ever ordered or even mentioned an X-ray. When I told him this, his wide, kind face furrowed, and he asked me to walk for him. Then he arranged me on the table to examine my leg. His first touch, on the outside of my upper leg, sent me through the ceiling. "You're going to radiology when you leave here," he said gently. "Then we'll go from there."

I was relieved and grateful to this man, who seemed genuinely caring about my condition, but

I didn't really expect much; I'd seen too many heads shake over the years about what couldn't be done to treat polio or its enervating aftermath. The next evening, I was getting dressed for a friend's book party when the phone rang. "I have your results," Dr. Ranere said, by way of introduction. "I'm looking at the X-rays. No wonder you're in so much pain. You have no hip left."

I grabbed a pen and started taking notes, an old habit from my years as a journalist that kicks in whenever I get bad news. "No hip," reads my scrawl on the back of an envelope. "Ball of hip is completely flattened. Bone on bone. Cysts, spurs, scarring. Severe degenerative arthritis. Total hip replacement."

I don't remember the rest of the conversation until its end, when Dr. Ranere asked if I had any questions. "Well, I have a lot of them," I said. "But the main one is—how do you feel about all this?" I don't know what made me ask this, though now it seems the best thing I could have asked him, and my candor may have taken him off-guard.

"To tell you the truth, I'm relieved," he told me. "If we were dealing with the effects of polio, we couldn't do anything about it. But we can fix this. The only thing that concerns me about a hip replacement for you is the rehab."

I went to the book party that night and made an effort to be sociable, even though I could barely make it up the driveway. My mind was reeling. I knew that I had been given extraordinary news: This new diagnosis, as common as rain, changed the facts about the recent past and the possibilities for the future. I had been limping around for a decade while friends worried and doctors shrugged, and yet the polio had been such a basic starting point that no one could see beyond it.

The dictum in medical training, drilled into the minds of prospective doctors, is "When you hear hoofbeats, think horses, not zebras." My medical history had presented the opposite problem. Polio, rare and specific, had been the zebra in range from the beginning, and that shadowy presence prevented anyone from thinking, *Well, heck, maybe there's a horse around here, too.* Until now.

So began my one-woman research project. Over the next several weeks I read so much about hip-replacement surgery—the approaches, failure rates, rehabilitation programs, recovery, and outcomes—that the data began to blur and threatened to become meaningless. The procedure has improved dramatically in the past two decades, and the patients lining up for it have increased accordingly: some three hundred thousand hip replacements are done each year in the United States alone. Everyone, it seemed, knew someone who knew someone. There is danger in this glut of commonality. As with pregnancy or grieving or torn rotator cuffs, strangers on the street are happy to predict your outcome. You must endure the tall tales of the man who played tennis five minutes after surgery, the woman whose aunt never walked well again. Euphemisms and horror stories and happy endings abound. There are videos and stories on Web forums that range from the terrifying to the miraculous. Hungry and hostage, I devoured them all.

Dr. Ranere had referred me to the orthopedics department of a nearby teaching hospital, and when I made an appointment, I was asked to bring a digital copy of my X-rays. I picked up the disc the day it was ready and drove home so that I could see it for myself. I knew no more than the average layman about reading an X-ray, but when the images came on the screen I gasped. Here was my "good" hip, the left one, its femoral ball of pearly white contained in its socket, surrounded by a dark-gray space of cartilage, which cushions joints and allows bones to move without knocking into one another. And then here was my other hip. It was an explosion of white. The image looked like a drawing from an anatomy book on one side and an overexposed negative on the other. The top of the femoral ball was as flat as a kitchen table, and it was flush against the pelvic socket that held it in place. I felt like I was shaking hands with my own history. *Oh, so there it is,* I thought. *There's a picture of all that pain.*

The intake questionnaire I was given in the waiting room had a special section, with seventeen descriptors for the type of pain the patient had experienced in the past six months: burning and piercing and shooting and constant and dull and throbbing. Being a word person, I appreciated these precise distinctions. I checked off eleven of the seventeen.

Dr. M. fit the standard surgical model: straightforward and laconic, gazing much more intently at my X-rays than at me. He called the damage "significant," confirmed what Dr. Ranere had told me, and said he could get me in for surgery within a couple of months. I asked him if he could tell how long this had been going on, and he shrugged. "More than five years, more like ten."

I asked him to quantify how bad my hip was. "You look at hundreds of X-rays a year," I said. "At one end of the spectrum you have a guy who can wait two years for surgery, at the other, someone who should book an O.R. tomorrow. Where do I fall?"

He didn't shrug this time. He said, "Most people with these X-rays would have gotten here a long time before now."

A standard X-ray is one of the most common and efficient tests in medicine. I'd lost count of the medical professionals I had seen regarding my leg over the previous twenty years. I was given exercises, referrals to physical therapy, pain-killers, brochures on cortisone shots, a sugges-tion from one professional to visit—her word—a cobbler. And yet no one, including me, had thought to suggest a test that takes ten minutes and generally costs a few hundred dollars.

I've always liked the joke about the loud-mouth whose tombstone reads YEAH, BUT I WAS RIGHT. I have a tendency to be that person—so attached to my own convictions that I can miss the wider or more nuanced story. I'd spent a lifetime trying to overcome the consequences of polio, and in so doing I'd shaped the narrative in a way that didn't leave much room for anything else. Dr. Ranere was the first medical profes-sional I'd seen in years who was less interested in my assumptions than in his own observations.

Of all the things I've learned from the realizations of the past few years—the hallelujah moment when I got a new diagnosis—one of the most important had to do with my own humility. With the idea that I didn't have to know the whole story, already iron-clad, didn't have to be the smartest person in the room. That sometimes the smartest person in the room is the one who says, "I have no idea."

An old friend used to say you could find out anything in the world with two phone calls: The first was to find out whom to call. I was lucky to live in one of the best medical communities in the world. My trip to Dr. M. had been an initial research foray, and I knew what was next.

More than a decade earlier, I had shared a two-family house with a young couple, a surgeon and an attorney, whose black Lab had grown up with Clementine; the three of us had been good friends and stayed in touch after we'd moved on. Now Marc was a highly regarded vascular surgeon at a top Boston teaching hospital. In the years we had shared a house (and dog care), I came to know him in particular and personal ways. He was as calm and considered as a redwood tree, and I trusted him utterly. I sent him a long email and hoped he would respond when he could; I already knew from talking to Jill, his wife, that he had to deal with hundreds of messages in a day.

Less than twenty-four hours later I had a reply. Marc had talked to colleagues and to people who worked in the O.R.; he had the name of the surgeon whom the surgeons went to see when they needed joint replacement. Within minutes I called Dr. Mattingly's office to make an appointment. His closest opening was four months away, in early July. From what I'd been told, that meant we would be scheduling surgery sometime in the fall.

I tend to research things small and large to the point of obsession, which is one reason my sister calls me a border collie. I had the opposite reaction after hearing from Marc. I felt free, as though I'd been given a pass on all that worrying and gone straight to the surgeon I needed. No second-guessing, no third and fourth opinions. Given that this was the man who would be taking a bone saw to my femur, it was a fairly critical decision. But from that day on I felt as though I'd been handed a map for the next part of my life. I didn't have to watch the procedure on YouTube, go to medical school, talk to four thousand people about what I was about to go through. I just had to hold on to my fear and wait it out.

14.

....

I met my surgeon on a hot morning in July, days after returning from Taos. For the first time in my traveling life I'd requested a wheelchair to get me from one gate to another. This concession was hard fought: I was prideful, and ashamed of my pride, and the airlines' staff did little to relieve my discomfort. At one gate I had to wait half an hour for a prescheduled wheelchair; at the next, the attendant wheeling me through the airport threw my carry-on suitcase on my lap and treated me like a piece of cargo. I was getting a twenty-minute glimpse at real disability, at the depersonalization and powerlessness that seems to go along with it, and any ambivalence I had about the impending surgery disappeared in a wave of gratitude. Unlike millions of people, I had a remedy available—an obvious fact that took a long time for me to comprehend, both leading up to the surgery and in the months following it. A compromised leg was my version of normal. To think that I could change that—that I might be one of those people thoughtlessly gliding from one place to another—was a conceptual challenge without a guidebook; it required a huge leap of the imagination.

• • •

A physician friend once pointed out that orthopedic surgeons tend to be hale and hearty because they need to be; theirs is the most physical of the surgical specialties. Dr. Mattingly was a friendly, handsome, take-charge man about my age who looked like the first-rate college football player he had been. He exuded confidence. He shook my hand warmly, turned to the X-rays waiting on the screen, and chuffed in response to what he saw. "Only one thing to do here!" he said. "You need a total hip replacement."

Later, I would be hit by the classic amnesia of medical encounters; if not for my notepad, I would remember very little of what we said that day. Typically, I had come armed with a list of questions—when I could swim and walk the dog were my most urgent and least medical—but most of them paled before Mattingly's authority. I knew enough about how surgeons think to realize he was telling me what mattered.

The next fifteen minutes were a blur of information: I would be on two crutches for six weeks, which he believed brought better long-term results. The prosthesis was uncemented, a better choice for more active patients. He would make a six-inch posterolateral incision on the side of my upper hip, then separate the strands of the gluteus medius to get to the femur. I would spend a day at New England Baptist Hospital doing pre-op, digital scans, and blood work, as well as donate my own blood weeks prior to the procedure. When I asked him if he had done the surgery on polio patients before, he answered yes, quietly, and I could tell from his answer he was being polite—it might have been like asking me if I was familiar with nouns and verbs.

It is testament to my naïveté, or denial, that I asked him the following question: "I have tendons and muscles that are tighter than those in a normal leg," I told him. Would it be helpful for him to know where they were and what their limitations were, in terms of positioning me during surgery? Mattingly looked at me as though I'd just offered to hold the scalpel, and he smiled. "Well, you're going to be asleep," he said gently, and when I still didn't get it, he added, "We can do anything we want."

Only then did I begin to allow for the anatomical assault of this procedure, one of the most common surgeries in the world and also one of the most aggressive. The hip and socket are exposed and the hip joint is dislocated (think turkey drumstick). The femoral head and stem are removed with a surgical bone saw. The acetabulum, the cup that rests in the pelvic socket and allows the leg bone to rotate, is power-washed to get rid of osteophytes, bone fragments, and cysts. The alignment of the hip is measured and remeasured for range of motion and optimal placement; the prosthesis is selected and tested for precise positioning. The surgical team replaces the acetabular cup and liner and drills out the remaining femoral bone to make room for the prosthesis, which is then hammered into place with a rubber mallet.

I knew most of this before I met Mattingly, but my mind chose to arrange the facts in a capsule of innocence, as though cheerful doctors and nurses were going to rearrange me like Legos, then give me a lollipop and a morphine drip. This was a helpful state to abide in for a while, just as it would be crucial later on for me to leave it behind, to absorb exactly what was being done to me and to what effect. But that morning I was a willing recruit; I made the necessary transfer of power to Dr. Mattingly within moments of meeting him. How much of my pain did he think this would address? About 95 percent. What kind of rehab could I expect? Ordinary. (Only this answer would prove too optimistic.) And finally, incredible though it seemed, he told me he could lengthen my leg— and reduce at least by half the discrepancy I had had since polio. In other words, since I had taken my first step.

The digital bone scan he was ordering would give him exact measurements of the leg; the polio, he believed, had left my bones alone.

"Your muscles are firing," he said. "From the X-rays, the bones are unaffected. You've been through rehab; you're motivated. I'm not worried about you. I'm worried about the guy who won't get off the couch and still thinks this will change his life."

My limp and my pain had been the two ways in which I'd been able to chart my decline, but probably more telling was the amount of muscular atrophy that had crept up on me in the past few years. Because my right leg was about 1.5 inches shorter than my left and the Achilles tendon was tight, my right foot couldn't really touch the ground if I straightened my left leg. I walked on my right toes to compensate, and this correction had gone from slightly cumbersome to dramatic in the past ten years. I had a photo on my refrigerator that Caroline had taken in the late 1990s, when we were in the White Mountains. I am standing with one leg on a rock, looking strong and happy. The leg is flexed; the calf is defined. When I found the picture, some years after she died, I thought it was my strong left leg. Then I realized it was my right leg. I was in my mid-forties, and my leg used to be strong, and now I could barely flex that muscle, and it looked like a different leg.

I shook Dr. Mattingly's hand, walked out to the front office, and scheduled surgery for the first date available, in November.

15.

....

I learned to row when I was forty-seven, the summer of 1998. An avid sculler for years, Caroline had convinced me to get in her racing shell one summer on a lake in New Hampshire, and the few strokes I managed sent my heart aloft. I came home and called Community Rowing, in Watertown, and signed up for beginning sculling classes. They were held on the serpentine Charles River, where novices had to share space with eight-person crews and zealous singles and the usual river population of kayaks and canoes. My class started out with eight people, but a week into it, the other woman my age dropped out. So now we were seven: two brawny men about my age, a pair of young women who had rowed crew together in college, a thirty-year-old yoga fanatic, a twenty-two-year-old former gymnast, and me.

I was the slowest and weakest rower in the boats. The coach, a good-humored man named John, paired me with Rachel, the gymnast; maybe he hoped her quads would make up for mine. We started off in huge wherries and graduated to tubby mid-size shells; we did sprints in pairs, rowing along beside each other, learning starts and turns and how to get back in the boat after capsizing. I became the guinea pig for this remount when I rowed enthusiastically into hidden weeds one afternoon and catapulted into the Charles. Because I was a lifelong swimmer and had already flipped once in Caroline's boat, this neither frightened nor deterred me. I had one trait that allowed me entrance into the rowing community: I was so stubborn they couldn't get rid of me. Rachel was tireless and the two men were driven—one a surgeon, the other a securities lawyer—and still I tried, day after day, to race them as we advanced to slender racing shells.

One day I sagged over my oars at the end of a sprint, disheartened, because the lawyer had creamed me once again. Rachel was impatient with my delusions. *"Gail,"* she said, the writing on the wall, "he has a back the size of your sofa." But I kept rowing, and rowing, and by the end of the summer I had deltoids I was proud of and I had bored Caroline on the phone each night with tales of my exploits. We rowed that year until late October, and John and I became fond of each other, though it was clear he didn't think I was racing material. One evening we were walking up the dock to the boathouse. "You know, John," I said, "there's one difference between me and the rest of the class you haven't noticed yet."

"Really?" he said.

"Yeah," I said, and grinned as I headed for my car. "Next summer, I'll still be here."

He laughed, and probably didn't give me a second thought. But I remember that moment, because fourteen years later, I'm still on the river, good days and bad, and I've never seen any of the rest of them again.

My beautiful old Van Dusen lightweight was Caroline's boat; she taught me to row in it and left it to me when she died. I talk to the boat, by which I suppose I talk to Caroline. "Hello, bunny," I usually say, once I have entered the cool, shadowy bay and reached toward it on its lower rack. "Hello, bunny, here I am"—which is silly, really, given that I think of the boat more as a horse than a bunny. Maybe I'm speaking to some ephemeral presence I count on—Caroline, the memory of her, the manifestation of her in the boat—to let them all know I am keeping up my end of the bargain. To keep going. To row the boat she can no longer row. To care for it, though not as well as she would—it is scuffed and doesn't get the polishing and fussing over that it did in her capable hands. After she died I swore I'd row until I couldn't anymore, and I set new goals every few years: to row until I turned sixty, or for ten years past her death, or for another hundred miles in a season. Her image on the water coached me: *How am I doing?* I asked, even as the rows dropped from seven miles to six miles and then, by the time the pain set in, to three or four. The summer after I'd found out about my hip, I modified my rowing vows to fit the news: I would finish out the season, and try my hardest to get in the thirty rows I needed to maintain my private boat rack.

Thirty rows in a season is a gentle quota for a fit rower, and I had maintained it for years without much effort. But these days people on the dock asked if I needed help carrying the boat. Nowadays, when I docked, I used an arm and my strong leg to hurl myself onto the dock with more sprawl than grace.

By late summer I knew I had to either push forward or give up and take a medical leave, which meant putting the boat into storage for the season. I started doing shorter rows, and as the light waned toward autumn every trip seemed like a victory—bittersweet and particularly beautiful, because, despite my surgeon's predictions, I was not convinced that I could do this after surgery. The river became the place where I could take my pre-op anxiety, which was showing up in devilish and displaced ways.

I felt scared and alone. For so long I had felt invincible: I used to swim the freshwater ponds on Cape Cod until October, following the perimeter if the place was deserted. If I got caught in a summer rain while I was rowing, I waited it out under a bridge or rowed through it; it was like being baptized from above. But these days I sent a cautionary alert to Nancy or Peter from the boathouse before I went out: "rowing— home in two hours." Now I did circles—a mile upstream, then two down, then back to the dock—instead of what I used to do, which was to row in one direction with heedless joy until I got tired.

One afternoon I went out on the river in a bad state. I was tired and worried about the surgery, and I had spent an hour the evening before immersed in a toxic pastime: Googling old boyfriends and pondering the road not taken. Thanks to the new world of knowing too much about anyone you ever met, this was hardly a revelatory activity, but that night I stumbled upon new data about two different men I had loved.

The first was a recent wedding announcement, the other an acknowledgment to a spouse in a book published years earlier. Both instances suggested the kind of wife I had never been and probably never *could* have been: both painted tableaux, at least in my mind, of flawless dinner parties and social hobnobbing and renovated barns in Greenwich or the like. I was lying on the couch in the living room when I read these tidbits, wearing gym shorts with my hair in a ponytail. Shiloh and Tula were lounging nearby; I was having leftover chicken for dinner and watching reruns of *Nurse Jackie*. Here was the life I had created, and whatever it was, it was not a flawless dinner party waiting to happen.

The next day, while I was rowing, I let my mind run free. This was an old and treacherous internal tape: I had forgotten to marry and have kids; I often preferred canine company to human; I would die sad and alone. Such was my recitation of despair, pulled out from time to time like an ill-shaped sweater you can't bring yourself to give away. My friend Jean had managed to interrupt some of the narrative on the phone the night before. "Really?" she asked, unimpressed by my former lovers' new mergers and acquisitions. "*Really?* Sorry. Can't see you renovating a barn for somebody else to write in."

So I flailed along, rowing my way toward hip surgery. After a couple of miles my demented script had faded, or maybe widened, to the larger truth, one without projections or fantasies about people I hadn't known for years. I was sixty and felt forty-five, I was dog-besotted and forgot to brush my hair, I liked AA meetings better than churches and forest walks more than restaurants. An unconventional life, but *my* life, and out of the blue that day, somewhere around mile three,

I started singing. "On the Street Where You Live." "Crazy." "Red River Valley." I rowed past kayakers and kids feeding the ducks from the shore, and I kept belting out songs with my passable second alto, a happy madwoman singing only slightly better than I rowed. When I got to the dock I was sweaty and hoarse, and I hauled myself out of the boat and lay there on the deck like a beached seal. And I, too often a self-accounting of imperfections and regrets, said aloud to myself, "You are so awesome." And for that moment, I completely was.

16.

···

In the weeks before surgery, my life became the ship of organization I had always longed for. I paid the bills and put my gym membership on hold. Tula's shots were updated, my teeth were cleaned. My freezer brimmed with decent one-zap meals. I rolled up the throw rugs (deadly for crutches), moved the houseplants inside, brushed the dog, and filled the pantry. I bought five thick novels and enough ibuprofen and lemon seltzer to stock a Red Cross tent. My friend Donna, an expert in public health, went with me to hip-replacement class at New England Baptist Hospital, where they handed out pens in the shape of a femur. I took four pages of notes with mine. We listened to surgical nurses and physical and occupational therapists; we learned how to get into and out of bed, climb stairs, carry dinner around one's neck while on crutches. There was a camaraderie with the other forty-plus people in the room, who looked to range in age from their mid-forties to their eighties. One of the youngest patients was a man who said he was forty-five and had been working three jobs for the past two years, in order to take off the time he needed to recover.

I made a list called Friends of Gail, both for my peace of mind and for letting people know I was OK. Then I looked at the list: neighbors and dog people and rowers and writers and AA people and women from the gym. So yes, they happened to be cooks and carpenters and therapists—everyone you'd ever need to run an island—but they were also full-hearted: someone you'd holler out for during a tornado, or walk through fire to save. It was as if God had said, "List the amazing people you know," and I did, and they turned out to be my friends, loyal and loving, and I was about to find out how much that was true.

Here were the realities and restrictions of the next few months: I lived alone in a two-story house with a fifty-five-pound young dog. I couldn't drive for six weeks or bend at the waist more than ninety degrees, and was directed to use two crutches for *every* step (their italics). I couldn't cross the vertical axis, or midline, of the body with my operated leg, or twist in any way that would rotate the hip. This restriction effectively keeps you in a straight line from rib cage to toes. To get into and out of bed, I had to use my strong leg as a crane to hoist the other one. I had a reach stick that could pick things up off the floor; a contraption with pulley straps that helped me put on compression stockings (a job that took thirty minutes the first time I tried, with Donna helping). I had a "dressing stick," a euphemism for a cruel little device for grabbing socks and shoes that, once tamed and befriended, becomes to the patient like fire or the wheel. I could not sweep the floor, pick up the newspaper, bend over to pet the dog. By the time I came home from surgery, my house was outfitted with a shower chair (later recalled!), a raised toilet, a walker Peter had found in his basement, exercise instructions in every room, crutches, canes, and seven gel packs in the freezer.

I suppose all of us consider our loved ones extraordinary; that is one of the elixirs of attachment. But over the months of pain and disrepair of that winter, I also felt something else that made the grimness tolerable: I felt blessed by the tribe I was part of. My fifties had been about loss: Caroline, my father and mother, then Clementine—all had died within a span of six years, almost to the day. Yet here I was, supposedly solo, and the real truth was that I had a force field of connection surrounding me.

When I had told Peter, months earlier, about what awaited me, I prefaced the news with a framework. Our brother-sister friendship is usually gruff and half-kidding, mostly about the dogs, so I send up a flare when deeper subjects are addressed. "I need to tell you something important," I said that day, all good cheer so as not to worry him. I hurried through the outline: what the X-rays had found, total hip replacement, crutches, months of rehab. Then I took a breath.

Peter looked expectant. "Well, the dog is covered," he said. "I've got that. But that's it, right? You don't have cancer or anything?"

It was pure Peter, an endearing moment that would repeat itself over the coming months with other friends and other needs: Oh, OK, got that. But that day I remember feeling the treasure of the unspoken—of brusque dialogue between friends whom you simply trust and count on. What Peter was saying was that he would walk Tula every day, in blizzards or rain or when he was tired, for several months and sometimes twice a day. For however long it took.

I finished my thirty rows at the end of September. I washed down the Van Dusen, now twenty-five years old, and settled it in its bay and told it aloud that I'd be back. Surgery was scheduled for mid-November, but the first week of October I got a call from Dr. Mattingly's office offering me a date three weeks earlier, and I grabbed it. The new date meant I got a jump on all that pre-op dread. That it was now going to happen on Halloween morning—one of my favorite holidays—seemed a good omen. Tula would go trick-or-treating with Shiloh and Peter and Pat while I was sleeping it off at New England Baptist. I spent five hours at the hospital for a preparatory visit: the digital bone scan, more X-rays, blood donation, meetings with social workers and occupational therapists and pharmacists who went over every detail. For two days I washed down my hip and leg with an antiseptic solution.

The night before surgery I had my final swim for at least six weeks and said good-bye to my throng of women at the gym. My friend Chris, an assistant swim coach, was a long-limbed, five-foot-eleven-inch physics teacher, so fast in the pool I called her "Neutrina." She declared that on my return I would be Titania, named after the high-tech components of my new hip. Originally connected by where we had landed in the locker room, my gym friends and I were now joined by stronger stuff: I'd gotten to know two different women when they lost their beloved dogs; I'd seen food drop-offs on the benches for a woman whose husband had suffered a stroke. We may have been there for the pool or the treadmill or Pilates, but the heart got a workout, too.

Another crucial stop before surgery was the AA meeting I'd routinely attended for twenty-seven years—a place that, from my experience, was such a bin of compassion that no fear was too much to take there. I'd stumbled in during the summer of 1984 and said, for the first time aloud, "I'm an alcoholic," then burst into tears; in the ensuing decades, I went there for a weekly dose of wisdom, courage, and high entertainment. AA broke down demographics of race and class and gender; a few blocks from Harvard, our meeting had regulars from the university, halfway houses, old Italian neighborhoods, South Boston, and the suburbs, and drop-ins from other countries. The elevator on the way up to the meeting had a sign engraved near its emergency button that read HELP IS ON THE WAY, and every time I saw it I smiled.

It would be weeks, probably months, before I was strong enough to get back here, so I was soaking up as much insight and hope as I could muster. But of all the advice and support I received, the one comment that stood out after surgery had come from a young guy who liked to remind people how tough he was. He'd had shoulder surgery a few years earlier, and the night I came to the meeting to say good-bye, he broke role long enough to slap me on the back as he was leaving. "Rehab sucks," he said, "but you gotta do it." And in every grueling exercise I did in the next few weeks, I could hear Richard goading me on.

My fears were amped up for a couple of reasons. The first was that I was going into this with muscles and mechanics compromised by polio, and no one—no surgeon or physical therapist or psychic—could forecast with certainty what or how much I would get back. I might wind up with a gladiator hip joint and a leg that still didn't work too well. The damage done over the past twenty years—the amount of time I could trace my decline—was a noticeable decrease in strength, flexibility, and endurance. I now walked up stairs with one leg and a handrail. My left leg did most of the work of walking; my right had become so weak it was a pivot and cane, following the left leg's lead. Musculature is what holds up the skeleton, and my internal scaffolding had all but collapsed.

It was a chicken-and-egg dilemma: Had the damage from polio been the causative agent in my hip's failure, or had my hip's breakdown been the reason for further muscle loss? This mattered greatly for one main reason: It would define how much strengthening and possibility I had before me. How well I could walk again. I wouldn't know this for months, and I knew I wouldn't know it, and that my leg—more than any doctor or prognosis—would be the one to tell me.

The other reason for my anxiety was that whatever denial I had used to get through the past few years had been abandoned. After my crash course in Dr. Mattingly's office that first day, I now needed to know precisely what the procedure entailed so that I could get into the psychic state to allow it. I was increasingly conscious of how protective I had always felt toward my right leg, which had worked so hard to keep up with its mate and suffered so many slings and arrows. I could be merciless about pushing onward: to swim farther, work harder, be a better person. Too often unforgiving, my inner voice was a tough coach even in a winning season. But my leg was always exempted from this severity, for reasons I am grateful for but do not understand. It was as though some split had happened long ago, creating some shelter, or conflict-free zone, in which the wounded part of me got a free pass.

Now I was about to let a group of miracle-working strangers put me under general anesthesia while they sawed off the top of my femur and built me a new chariot. I looked at the diagrams in online medical journals about the complexity of placement and range of motion; I read about the body's natural defense to trauma. I was terrified, but I knew myself well enough to walk toward the terror, so that I could embrace what was about to happen to me instead of flee it.

The surgery was on a Monday. The previous evening, after I swam laps until I was too tired to think, I came home and devoured a last meal, fortifying myself with roast chicken and vanilla ice cream. I got a final call from the hospital telling me to be there at 7 a.m. Avery, who lived at the end of the block, was driving me. At dawn I put baskets of peanut-butter cups on the front porch for the trick-or-treaters and kissed Tula on the head; Nancy, who was next door, would come get her within the hour. Avery was on the first shift: Dr. Mattingly would call her when surgery was over to tell her how things went, and Jean would meet me when I was out of recovery, sometime in the afternoon.

I had had no food or water since midnight, and a couple of people had warned me about the potential backup in the O.R. "Oh, God," one alleged well-wisher said. "If they have an emergency, you could be there all day, with nothing to eat or drink." That became my focus and worst fear, dismissed when they took me into pre-op an hour early. I gave up my contact lenses and got the obligatory johnny, and they must have given me something else, too, because I remember only vague, pleasant snatches after my first moments in the room. Avery tells me I flirted with the chief of anesthesiology, a soft-spoken bear of a man about my age who took my hand as he explained his plan. When Dr. Mattingly appeared he clapped his hands and said, "Let's do this!" He signed my leg with a flourish, a standard procedure I found comforting as well as symbolic. I was to be his canvas for the next few hours. The nurse at my side was wearing a Halloween necklace of plastic skulls, which delighted me. I touched her arm and said, "I have one question: What music are you guys going to listen to?"

She grinned and said, "The Beatles!" and I gave her a thumbs-up, and the next thing I knew I was in a hospital bed and it was over, and I was looking at Jean's shining blue eyes.

17.

....

Here is the official surgeon's report from that day.

Date of Procedure: 10/31/2011
Preoperative Diagnosis: Osteoarthritis
   right hip with polio residuals
Postoperative Diagnosis: Osteoarthritis
   right hip with polio residuals
Name of Procedure: Right Total Hip
   Replacement

PROCEDURE: General anesthesia and endotracheal intubation, 2 grams of IV Kefzol, Foley catheter, lateral decubitus position, routine prep and drape. Posterolateral incision, posterior approach, dislocation posteriorly osteotomy made of the neck. The head and neck removed. Limited anterior superior capsulectomy was performed. Osteophytes were removed from the acetabulum, which was then reamed to 53 mm. A 54 mm. cup was placed in 40 degrees of abduction, 20 degrees of forward flexion and secured with two dome screws and a neutral liner. A 36 liner was chosen because of the patient's history of polio with weakness to the right lower extremity. Attention was directed to the femur, which was then prepared and trial reduction performed. The real implants were then inserted with the stem in 25 degrees of anteversion, sleeve in 20 degrees of anteversion. The femoral head was applied, the hip reduced and found to be stable to extremes of range of motion with a combined forward flexion sign between 40 and 45 degrees. The +6 head was chosen in order to gain length since the patient was 3 cm. short by scanogram but had a flexion contracture of her ankle. We gained approxi-mately 1.5–2 cm. in length. The wound was thoroughly irrigated and closed in layers with the posterior capsular and external rotator repair being performed.

What is often most dramatic to the body can be of less interest to medical professionals, particularly on a post-surgical ward. They know to expect edema, mild fever, anemia, precipitous drops in blood pressure, nausea, howling pain. All these are considered treatable but not significant—which is to say that they are normal, will go away, and are not usually indicative of anything dangerous or extraordinary.

I needed four transfusions in the first twenty-four hours after surgery, probably a result of my being small-framed and thus with less blood to lose and replace safely. My oxygen levels were too low; my blood pressure was 80 over 40, and I swooned every time I got up. My hematocrit, which measures the amount of red blood cells in the blood, was about half what it should have been. The concept of food was exquisite, the reality unbearable. A plate of meat loaf, once summoned, had all the appeal of stewed tire.

These details were alarming only to me, and then not very, because for a couple of days I was in a Disney world of peace and love, also known as a central line of morphine. I have a vague memory of walking the first night, and hollering from another stratosphere as I did. My leg was the size of a rugby player's. To get in and out of bed I had to use my strong leg as a forklift for the right one. People—friends and nurses and physical therapists—came and went in the most routine fashion, but to me each event seemed monumental, a choreography of intrigue and hope. I told my physical therapists how much I loved them. I repeatedly plugged my cell-phone charger into the wall reserved for the cardio monitors; amazingly, no nurse tried to smother me with a pillow.

Even in the aftershock of surgery, I knew somewhere that all this acute melodrama was just that—the heightening of the banal that is the essence of the post-op experience. What stood out, though, in those first few days of illusory urgency, was the sound of Dr. Mattingly's voice, coming to me across a great sea as he stood at my bed at 6 a.m. the day after surgery.

"Things went *very* well," he said. And then: "We were able to lengthen the leg by about one and a half to two centimeters, or five-eighths of an inch."

Long after that brief conversation in the dark, I still feel the relief and awe that his words evoked. "We were able to lengthen the leg . . ."— like saying, *We were able to walk on water,* or, *We were able to lift the moon.* I knew exactly, even in a morphine cloud, how vast and how little five-eighths of an inch was: It was going to be my golden mean.

Dr. Mattingly left that morning to make his rounds, and his surgical physician's assistant stayed to give me the full report. They had found "a real mess" inside, she told me; it was much worse than the pre-op screens had suggested. "You *had* to do this," she said. I let go of her hand and entered the land of post-op bliss. I had had to do this, and now it was done.

I have notes and exercise sheets and post-op instructions from those first few weeks, all meticulously organized by Jean and Nancy, and I can look at them now and remember the intensity that every detail held. To the patient, it feels as though some grand odyssey is unfolding, with a cast of one. It is the body, perfect machine, showing off its stuff. If everything is working right, it reacts to the major assault of surgery by becoming Luke Skywalker: Fluid rushes in and cells regenerate and muscles and nerves regrow. I was stunned by this drama, and humbled, and in the early days at home I learned that my will had little agency in the way the story unfolded.

Anatomical functions I had taken for granted revealed themselves with bells and whistles. When I stood I could feel the blood whooshing through my body as my blood pressure changed; when I walked a few steps, my heart raced and I was short of breath. I had no appetite but began to crave protein, like a great bear gathering resources. I'd hardly eaten during my days in the hospital, and had gained thirteen pounds of water weight, all of it from my waist to my toe.

More radical was the leg itself—the way it felt, the way it worked, the way my brain accepted so much new information. I remember thrusting my foot up and outward the first morning I was home, trying to accommodate the feeling of this longer, floppy limb, and I had the image of a foal standing for the first time, its long legs goofy and in the way until they got their bearings. I couldn't limp the old way even if I'd wanted to; there was too much leg there now.

The length Dr. Mattingly had gained in rebuilding my hip only hinted at my uprightness in the world, an ease and agency I glimpsed but couldn't believe. For years my body had leaned toward its weakest point. Now it was as though someone had put a shim under a bureau, so that the entire structure was stable. I didn't know yet that all the rest of my leg would have to play a long and painful catch-up—that nerves and muscles and tendons and ligaments would have to stretch, tear, readjust. For now I had only the sweet realization that I had been catapulted upward in the world. I was Alice eating the mushroom in Wonderland, and I felt powerful as well as tall: an instant dose of happy, to go up against the challenges of the next year.

It was nice to have these stoned epiphanies to appreciate, given the state I was in. Despite the transfusions, I was so weak I grew faint with almost no warning, and my newly arranged femur and leg had finally woken up to post-op pain. As my physical therapist warned me that first morning home, I had a few weeks of horrible ahead of me. But I also had Nancy, who came in and out continually, bearing the unflappable strength and good cheer of a doctor on *M*A*S*H*. She was tireless, she was hilarious, and somehow she had volunteered for this particular combat zone. And I had Peter running point with the canine unit—special ops in every way.

Standard protocol for a hospital release after hip surgery includes being able to climb six stair steps on crutches, and get yourself onto and up from a bed. This is pretty basic stuff. It does not include feeding yourself, answering a phone, picking up a newspaper, locking a door, pouring water in a dog's dish, or making a cup of coffee. These, I learned in my first days home, are high-functioning talents, and anyone who pulls them off without occasional whimpering deserves a good-conduct medal, or at least a merit badge.

Any change that matters, or takes, begins as immeasurably small. Then it accumulates, moss on stone, and after a few thousand years of not interfering, you have a glen, or a waterfall, or a field of hope where sorrow used to be. You have a second chance, or an unexpected kindness, or a voice singing somewhere that floods you with light. You have a leg that works a little better than you ever believed possible.

But there's always that moment, only a blink from the sacred to the mundane, when you think, *Oh, Christ, I have wasted it all.* I remember sitting on my couch in the dark one night when Caroline was dying, when I knew the gig was up, and thinking, *I want to change my life,* and of course we all think that, and then we don't. It's like trying to turn an ocean liner around and using a fork for a fulcrum. We just plug along and try not to mess up too badly.

Real change, though, is forgiving enough to take a little failure, strong enough to take despair in small doses. The ocean liner turns two degrees: different destination. You just don't drink for one day. Don't take the bait, load the gun, say the stupid thing. Do make the phone call, throw away the shoes that hurt. Just rest a little and then move another few inches down the path. When I was getting stronger I told a friend I felt like I was painting the kitchen floor with a watercolor brush: The point was never to look up.

David, Tink's husband, had had a hip replacement a year ahead of me. Wise and kind David, who called regularly throughout my post-op ennui to cheer me on. "There will come a time when you'll miss the old leg," he told me one winter night, a piece of counsel that rang true for months afterward. He knew, I think, that we attach ourselves to our familiar miseries, an easier act sometimes than striking out for the territory. This is a sad truth, though not insurmountable: Despair and fear do not disappear overnight when the conditions that wrought them have changed.

But here's something else I learned from all

the work and frustration of that first year: Strength is how you keep yourself from falling. With two good legs, when you start to fall, you can catch yourself.

I am standing in my living room in Cambridge, Massachusetts, and talking to my friend Stan, a former thoracic surgeon whose Alabama accent makes everything sound better. My visual perspective is so much higher than the last time I saw him that I laughingly pretend I'm as tall as he—about six feet—when I hug him hello.

As we talk, I try to get my hands around what I've been through. The past few weeks have been filled with distress and pain and occasional triumphs of possibility, and because I am so early in recovery from major surgery, I don't know yet what it means. "I don't know if what's happened to me is a big deal or a little deal," I tell Stan. "But whatever it is, I don't want to miss it—I don't want to turn away from this gift."

Stan comes over and puts his hands on my shoulders. "Are you kidding?" he says. "It's *huge.* It affects the entire notion of self."

18.

....

There is, of course, a dog story in all this—
adjacent dramas in Tula's world and mine. I
will try here to be a reliable narrator, given that
I am interpreting for us both.

Tula had been staying next door with Nancy
and her family for the time I was in the hospital.
The plan was that Nancy would bring Tula over
to see me the first evening, then home for good
the next day. So once I was set up in the
downstairs guest room, in they came.

Tula heard my voice from the back door—
"There's my girl!" I cried—and she ran into the
bedroom, ears back and eyes happy. She licked
my face—excitedly at first. Then she got a whiff
of what I'd been through, and she panicked. She
looked away, her tail went down, and she got
behind Nancy. When I spoke to her or called her
name, her ears flattened but she averted her eyes,
as though I were a predator, or a wounded human
who smelled of blood and trauma. Then she
started pulling toward the back door.

Now this seems straightforward and not all that
mysterious. I knew of similar incidents, where

friends had returned from a hospital visit to a dog who avoided them for days. And I knew from simple observation that Tula was terrified.

Dogs lead with their noses; they can smell another dog's fear, illness, or aggression from half a block away. Their discernment and powers of smell are several orders of magnitude greater than ours, which is why we use them as seizure dogs, bomb-sniffing dogs, search-and-rescue dogs. Recent studies suggest their ability to detect cancer in humans before it shows up on medical tests. They know so much with their sense of smell that we don't even know yet what they know.

I had a six-inch incision on my upper hip. When Tula ran up to me, she was banking on all the other sensate givens: her home, her human, my voice and affect. Then she smelled my wounded leg, probably my fear, plus a hundred hospital odors I can only guess at. Maybe she thought she was next. Months later, I would see her behave exactly the same way when Shiloh came back from a minor surgery.

Whatever part of me understood Tula's response, I couldn't absorb it with any equanimity. When I think back on all the misery of that first week home, this incident—a beloved dog turning away in fear—was the worst of it. I told Nancy to take Tula back to her house, and after they left, I broke down. Standing in the kitchen on crutches, I cried in Jean's arms like I hadn't cried through any of the past year. I wailed. I had let strangers carve me up like a grapefruit, and now Tula, frightened witness to this travesty, wanted none of it. For all the friends and flowers and casseroles waiting for me when I got home, I felt like an abandoned waif.

Tula reappeared the next afternoon, after a long walk with Peter and Shiloh. I was in a chair in the living room, and she ran up to me, slightly frantic in her shows of affection. Then she curled up across the room with me in her sight line, and slept as though in a coma.

It took a while for her to come around—to believe that I was still here, hadn't been replaced by some alien creature with metal wings. The crutches were less unsettling to her than my inertia and weakness, and my having upended the spatial truths about our lives. The second night I was home, Donna slept over, and Tula went upstairs to my bedroom with her—a gesture I took as a herding instinct to keep an eye on the whole house. But even after I felt able to stay alone, she kept up her quiet, vigilant routine. At the end of each night, when I was in bed in the downstairs guest room and Nancy had made a final walk-through, Tula circled the first floor as though doing a dorm check, stopping at my doorway and looking at me. Then she slowly climbed the stairs. I could hear her walking overhead to my room, hear her pausing, probably near the bed, then curling up in her usual spot. She slept there alone each night for that first week, as though she were waiting, uncertain but loyal, for the real me to come back home.

Then something happened that changed my need-ridden, human interpretation of my dog's behavior. I started sleeping upstairs again after a week. The first night, just after I had turned out the lights, Tula ran from the bedroom to the front windows and started barking—a ferocious, guard-dog bark I had heard only a few times, and always at perceived predators in the woods. This was a bark she had used once on a giant Newfoundland when she was young, and the bark she'd summoned at a faraway coyote. She ran from window to window, ignoring my calls to stop, and the barking was so intense and unrelenting I was certain she had seen a coyote or wild turkey on the lawn—rare but not implausible. Finally she went downstairs and made a last round of barking through the front and side of the house, then came back up and lay down beside me.

A couple of days later, Emily, Nancy and Jim's fourteen-year-old daughter, came over to see me. We were pals, which is to say that she would tell me the following story without editing.

"Did you hear a bunch of noise in your

driveway late the other night?" she asked. My driveway abutted theirs; whatever one of us heard, both of us heard. "Two boys I know were trying to come to my window," Emily said. "They said they came down the driveway and tried to get me to wake up, but that there was this ferocious dog in the upstairs windows who was going crazy."

So those were the predators Tula was after: two harmless teenage boys, looking for the girl next door. For any Samoyed to look ferocious is an act of extreme camouflage. I live in a walkers' neighborhood, where people come and go on my street at all hours. As far as I knew, my dog had never barked at a human passerby in her life. But with me flat on my back, Tula stepped up and became the mother bear of us all.

We got better on parallel paths. She walked next to me in the house, an undulating wave of white, while I made my way from room to room on crutches. A physical therapist came three mornings a week, and Tula lay in the foyer like a slab of marble while we walked outside. On stairs she stood next to me on the landing, serene and implacable, until I found the energy to go ahead. When I took a shower, she either curled up on the bathroom floor or poked her head inside the shower curtain, and tried to lick my wounded leg.

People moved through my house and state of mind, a parade of comfort. They dropped off lasagna, soups, chicken, homemade smoothies. Even from my state of bearable misery, I knew my life resembled a sitcom, with food arriving at the front door and sometimes going out the back, to replenish Nancy's family. There were dogs underfoot and Nancy toodling "Hellooooo!" as she let herself in, and Jean rearranging the mail and refrigerator as though these were tasks of pleasure. We had hung a sign on the front door reading PLEASE DO NOT RING BELL—IT WILL SET OFF THE DOGS, assuming that would send the right message to burglars as well as friends. Only Peter systematically ignored this instruction, even though he had helped write it; he figured that now when the bell rang, I would know who was about to charge inside. My old friend Pete came over and raised the bed in the guest room with a carpenter's act of levitation, and Donna elevated the sofa cushions in the living room, making the couch into a wacky-looking daybed-throne. I lay among the happy chaos, a stoned queen with her reach-stick scepter, wondering how I got so lucky.

It astounds me to consider the care I had. I can be temperamentally dark; gratitude samplers do not hang in my kitchen. But friendship—not a cynical or skeptical bone in my body. Maybe this absolute embrace comes from my having had and lost Caroline; I know now that our friendship was something precious and unfounded, a grace note with my name on it, and so her death has become a part of me and my ongoing narrative and touched everything else I love: as though she knew no one could replace her, so she sent me a whole truckload of friends to help me through.

Some of my luck was geographical. I live in a neighborhood that resembles a village—parks and ponds and rivers within a half-mile radius, groceries and shops a few blocks away. The crooked sidewalks are as well traveled as the streets they border. Everyone walks, especially dog people, on their way to the reservoir or the river. After a decade of living here, I was on a first-name basis with half the people on our long city block.

I also know that my living alone had a huge impact on the help I got, and not simply because people think, "Oh, she's solo; she needs a hand." It's because solitude itself makes you stretch your heart—the usual buffers of spouse and children are missing, so you reach toward the next circle of intimacy. I've appreciated this distinction for years: Single people form different depths and kinds of attachments with their principals, partly because of the time and space being vacated where a partner might have stood. If my little milieu included a dog and a spouse, none of my experience—Jean fielding calls and Tink marching down the street in her apron, looking like Mrs. Dalloway, and me lounging about with my crutches and complaints—would be even close to the same. Instead there might be a heroic husband taking care of everything, or an ambivalent spouse dealing with her own care-taker issues, or a teenage son stealing my painkillers or deciding to go to medical school. Romantic partners and offspring always get first shot at being the main characters, and inevitably they change the plot around. Happens every time.

19.

....

The bad times were at night, when fatigue felled me like a tree. God knows I had plenty of rescues: drive-by cheeseburgers and shower spotters and food drops that saved me, body and soul. But I longed to be able to do the simplest things: to cook a meal or empty the trash or (most of all) stride across a room. I was getting a crash course in what it felt like to grow old or infirm, and I kept thinking of my parents, of moments past when I realized what they could no longer do: my father's inability to get up from a chair but refusal to succumb to a walker, my mother using one arm to lift the other on her bad days from arthritis. I had viewed them as stubborn during these times, when I tried to help and they soldiered on. Now I applauded them, and regretted my impatience.

My solitary meals were valiant and pathetic efforts. It took me forty-five minutes to manage a plate with heated food, ice compresses for my leg, a fork, water, a phone, and crutches, all in one place. I couldn't lean or bend more than ninety degrees, so I had a ladle for dog food and a pitcher to pour water toward the bowl on the floor. I learned to throw things at the sink from my post at the counter: avocado pits or banana peels or seltzer bottles. Despair was too often a partner at these dinners, at least in the first six weeks, when I had been told to use two crutches with every step and I was too weak to break the rules even if I'd wanted to. My goals had never been so measured: to get to the counter, get to the couch, get to the end of the day.

This bleak corridor did not go on forever, though at the time I felt, beyond all rational thought, that it would. Humbled by how weak I was, I had neither the patience nor the faith to believe I would be strong again: might lift a boat or even carry a bag of groceries. Once I got to my bedroom, upstairs at the back of the house, I felt a relief bordering on bliss: crutches tucked nearby, safe for another day, nowhere else to go.

When I was strong enough, I climbed the stairs on crutches with my laptop in a backpack. The first few weeks my heart raced with exertion when I reached the top of the stairs, no matter how slowly I went, and I stopped there until I was sure I wasn't dizzy. Then I'd go a little farther—as far as the middle room, where the thermostat and lights were—and one night I stood there in the semi-dark, my hand on the wall, and said aloud, "You can do this."

It was the same voice I used for the dogs, for Clemmie and then Tula and Shiloh and every other dog I'd known, when they were scared or sick or trying to make a jump. *"You're OK. You can do it."* A reassurance from someone stronger, someone who knew. The voice a mother uses on the playground.

I didn't think much about this, that I was talking to myself and what a voice of consolation it was, until later. One afternoon a good friend had come to visit, and we were talking in the kitchen, with Peter nearby on a phone call. Lane asked me how I was, really and truly, and so I told her that I was all right but that sometimes it was awful, and then I told her about standing there in the dark until I was ready to keep going. Only when I finished did I realize that Peter, who always got the tough version of how-I-really-was, was no longer on the phone and had been listening behind me. And he said, quietly, "You are walking across Kansas."

In the medical dramas and miracle resurrections of popular culture, rehabilitation—the patient's incremental march toward well-being—is usually put on fast-forward. The triple bypass is performed; the man is seen shooting hoops with his son. High drama doesn't much lend itself to rehab, where the glories are micro-measured and repetition is the overriding story. Leg lifts? OK, do that ten thousand times and we'll reassess.

And yet it was here, on the living room floor or on a yoga mat by the pool or lying prone on a physical therapy table, that my real story unfolded, its thrills and crevasses exaggerated by the desertlike sameness of the work itself. The things I longed to do became the things I believed I would never do again, and this fear was so complete that I would hurl myself at the challenge with not a little desperation, then overshoot it and have to readjust. My surgeon cleared me to swim at six or seven weeks, and the first time I swam I went to the gym with the goal of putting my suit on, nothing more. Navigating on crutches from car to locker room and managing a swimsuit change took about twenty minutes. But then I made it to the wide steps of the pool and a lifetime of watery memories reached up for me, and I fell in like a drunken mermaid. I was so happy—so enveloped and no longer precarious—that I had to force myself to leave. When I got home, I went to sleep sitting up in a chair.

Time is a vast place when you are standing still. It was three months before I walked without crutches or cane, six months before I moved through the world with a shred of confidence. The first several weeks of winter I lay on the couch with my leg elevated and watched the walkers outside the window on my street—thoughtless bipeds on their way to someplace else, their limbs moving in seemingly perfect symmetry. I spied on everyone I knew, too: Peter's loping stride, Pat's easy marathoner's pace, Nancy's tireless gait. All of them seemed to possess the grace of dancers. At night, when the window show was over, I went to websites on walking and online orthopedic journals to read about how normal bodies achieved this vital, gliding phenomenon. "I hear it's a miracle surgery," people sometimes said, when hearing what I'd been through. Generally I smiled and appeased them. Yah, I thought to myself, still waiting here for the miracle.

My surgeon's discharge instructions were to "walk 4–6X a day, for 5 to 10 minutes. Walk outside if possible." The point was to get the patient moving, and trips to the microwave didn't count. But at the time I interpreted the advice as four to six real treks a day, and my heart sank at my anticipated defeat. Most people recover from hip replacement with the same leg they started with, but mine was on its maiden voyage, longer now but unschooled, and I couldn't go far without muscle spasm or fatigue. I was crutching around the house most of the day, so I aimed for one or two walks outside. The first time I emerged, blinking in the sun like the men in Plato's cave, my neighbor Rita came onto her porch and cheered.

Off I'd go, at first with a partner who could

spot me, eventually alone, the stopwatch running on my cell phone. New England was having the mildest winter in a decade, and I headed down the front steps in gym shorts and compression stockings and running shoes and a down jacket. I cannot imagine how odd I looked, though people forgive a lot when you are on crutches. Two houses, then three. Five houses, then turning around and seeing the ocean of distance back to my front porch. Finally to the little park halfway down the street—populated most days by me and a couple of stalwart mothers with their preschoolers.

One afternoon I saw a toddler at the park who was entranced by my crutches, and, with his mother hovering, he came toward me—step, lurch, step, lurch—with his arms out and a big smile on his face. He was fifteen months old, his mother said. "You're better at this than I am," I told him, and in a way I was in earnest, watching his every move. Spying on a toddler to learn the body's genius, to learn how to do it right. All moxie, he thrust himself into space, certain that it would receive him; his arms and torso took him forward while his legs figured out the mechanics. It was an amazing sight, that cold sunny day in December, and the image stayed in my mind's eye for months, as my body followed suit.

Walking, it turns out, is a mansion of complexity, and I know this mostly because I did it crookedly for so long. My lengthened leg now reached the ground without a built-in drag; it was as though two horses harnessed together, one smaller and slower, had finally been started from even gates. Every muscle from my toes to my rib cage hollered out in protest. Most of them were being stretched and torn as I reached that new distance; a few may never have been engaged at all.

The first several months I suffered shin splints and back pain and calf cramps and iliotibial band syndrome; if my foot landed in the wrong way while I was reinventing myself, I felt it later in my knee. I found a note that I wrote myself in winter that describes my state of mind. "I am frustrated and sick of it," I wrote, "aware that it is much much worse than people said it would be—and about precisely what I thought it would be. The weakness of my leg has made this a brutal rehab."

Occasionally I experienced the fundamental shift of my body as a visual hiccup while the world righted itself. Even in pain and in training, I could walk faster and better than I had in years. The first time I took a familiar walk at the reservoir, around a little peninsula, I looked out over the water and it seemed, just for a second, as though I were in a slow-moving car. That was when I knew—one of the times I knew—that the physics of my being in the world had changed. It was as though God kept throwing me a bone once in a while, just so I would keep going.

Thus did Kansas reveal itself, with endless plains and then dips and rises. The milestones I worried over came on their own: first swim, first walk in the woods with the dogs (I had Nancy, and one crutch), first trip to the store. For outpatient physical therapy I found a wry, lanky man who coached high school girls' basketball when he wasn't working on people like me. He was the perfect fit for me, kind and a bit of a wiseass, and he spent most of his energy convincing me to slow down and accept where I was. "They never tell you how bad it is," he said about joint replacement. "They're afraid you won't do it." I held on to his wrists and tried to walk on my heels, the same way I had with my mom when I was four. I cursed and complained; he put weights on my ankles and, later, slabs of icy gel packs on my leg. By the time he booted me, I half-worshiped him, because he had shown me the hallway to my own strength.

My micro-victories were how I survived months of uncertainty. On a Monday in May I said to my friend Morgan, "I'm afraid I'll never row again," and the words, typically melo-dramatic, so scared me that I drove to the boathouse the next day to see if I could lift the boat, and did. "You gotta have the want-to," a famous rodeo guy said about how he kept winning, and sometimes I think that was all I had, the want-to. I made it to the locker room, the boat bay, the first upstream bridge. That's good— now do that ten thousand times. My world became so focused that Jean began referring to it over the summer as Camp Gail. "So what happened at Camp Gail today?" Pleased to be recognized as my own zealous director, I named her honorary camp counselor.

With uncemented hip replacement, the first three to six months are critical, because the bone is growing into the prosthesis. After the early months of rehab, Dr. Mattingly told me I could do anything except run (no worries there) or leap from a high table (ditto). As I worked and fretted my way toward getting stronger, I kept being reminded that the body has its own intelligence, an elegant circuitry that all but bypasses conscious thought. Sometimes no matter how fierce my want, my leg would falter, or muscles would spasm, or fatigue would level me, and on those days I wanted to weep over my limited return. Walking was still harder than anything else; my muscles and tendons were trying to catch up to my smooth-gliding joint.

I was plodding along a path one afternoon, frustrated with how labored and unnatural my movements felt, and I thought, *OK, pay attention to the good leg,* and then I realized how obvious this simple instruction was. I had been trying to dictate the mechanics of my right leg, without much luck, and so I gave a new instruction: *Don't pay attention to me,* meaning my brain and my will and my effort to drive the chariot. *Just do what the other leg is doing.*

And it worked. Haltingly, but more smoothly than any effort of will could have achieved, my leg started moving in tandem with its partner. Like two dogs in harness, each of whom has to figure out what the other is doing. It was a moment in which I felt stunned and humbled and smart, smart in the sense that I had gotten out of my own way, and if it seemed a bit psycho—woman walking alone, talking to leg— well, at least my audience of muscles seemed to be listening. The mind-body dyad had revealed itself as the fragile, sometimes beautiful collaboration it is.

The polio virus destroys neurons, which carry signals from the brain to muscles to make them fire. Once the wires are down, the signal reroutes to another muscle—an efficient mechanism that can have unfortunate long-term side effects. The muscles that take over keep working and getting stronger and eventually overtaxed; the weaker one loses what feeble ability it had. There were lots of times in my life, most acutely in physical therapy, when I had been made achingly aware of this neurological shutdown: moments when I tried with all my might to isolate a muscle and it simply wouldn't fire, or was too weak for me to feel its effort. It was like being paralyzed, though on a smaller scale. I remember staring at my leg, feeling everything around the targeted muscle trying to help, and getting nothing back.

Now I had a different place to start from. The additional length Dr. Mattingly had given me had partly leveled the playing field—and had sent my right leg to the gym just by my walking across the room. The act of weight-bearing that was now possible engaged muscles from my waist to my toes that hadn't worked in years. I had months of this careful testing ground ahead of me, miles garnered and muscles emerging and protesting, but I couldn't know that yet; I had to bank on what little I had and the belief that I had a fighting chance.

About six months after surgery, I was sprawled in my usual place on the living room floor, trying to stretch and work individual muscles while Tula rolled a tennis ball my way. My routine was to do the easy, gratifying exercises at the beginning and end, so that the ones I hated—the ones that hurt, or, worse, where nothing happened—were buried in the middle. In this way did I trick myself from getting too discouraged.

That evening I wiggled a couple of toes—I was

strengthening my foot as well—and I felt the movement all the way up to my hip. I looked at my leg and tried the motion again, and I saw something move on the outside of my lower leg. It was the tibialis anterior muscle, and I'd never seen its definition before. My muscle's Rip Van Winkle moment. I wiggled my toes and it fired and moved and my heart soared. I was teaching my leg to walk again, except this time it was nearly two centimeters longer and I was sixty-one years old, and my first coach had been dead for six years.

20.

....

In the last year of my mother's life, in 2005, I flew to Texas seven times; three of those trips I was convinced it was the end. After my father died in 2003, she had stayed put in the brick colonial where they'd lived for forty years. She cooked a ham for herself on Easter Sunday and had a woman in to help her several times a week, with two daughters hovering by long-distance, and though she was ninety-one and barely weighed a hundred pounds, she insisted she was fine and could live on her own. My sister had long called her Little Mother as an endearment, and one winter day I walked into the house—I had driven from Santa Fe, New Mexico, where Pam lived—and Mom was standing in the kitchen, smiling in greeting and holding on to the table, so I wouldn't see that she was unsteady on her feet.

"Tiny Mother, where are you going?" I said, because she had clearly lost weight, and without a pause she pointed her cane skyward and said, "Up to heaven, I hope, to be with Bill."

· · ·

I was there for a three-day visit, and the next afternoon when I had gone for a swim, she called me on my cell and said, "Come home— something isn't right." When I got there she was sitting on the brick hearth by the fireplace, trying to talk but having trouble finding words. I called my father's former neurologist and told the office assistant that I thought my mother was having a TIA, or transient ischemic attack, which is what they call the little strokes that afflict the elderly. The woman put me on hold and when she came back in a few seconds, she said the doctor could see my mom in two weeks. I swallowed my rage and dialed my therapist, a psychiatrist, two thousand miles away. Within moments, on his instruction, I had given my mother an aspirin and told her we were going to the hospital to have her checked out. Halfway there she said, "I'm scared," which may be the only time I heard her say that in more than fifty years.

Her blood pressure was skyrocketing—220 over 120—and by the time we got her admitted, she was going in and out of lucidity. She was convinced that my father was in the room, which seemed to make her happy. The cardiologist took me in the hall and shook his head, and so I sat on the bed with her for hours, and finally, because I couldn't think of anything else to do, I started reciting Scripture, which I knew she loved. I got all the way through the Twenty-Third Psalm, to my surprise, and then I said, out of nowhere, "I shall lift up mine eyes to the hills, from whence cometh the Lord." It was a misquote from another psalm, but that was the best I could do, and we stayed there together until she nodded off.

Two days later, she was stable and seemed lucid but still couldn't talk, and after several planning sessions with my sister, I flew back to Boston to take care of things at home, with the idea that Pam and I would start the arrangements for assisted living. Monday morning my phone rang and I saw the hospital number and grabbed the phone, assuming it was the nurses' station.

"Hi, Gail!" my mother said brightly. "What are you doing?"

Her speech was normal, and she sounded about seventy years old. I tried to hide my amazement and so asked her questions that were fashioned to gauge her clarity. "Do you remember my being there?"

"Of course!" she countered.

"Do you remember my saying the Twenty-Third Psalm?" I asked.

"Oh, yes," she said happily. "You sounded just like a country preacher."

Then she told me the speech therapist had already been by that morning and was pleased by her progress. "I knew I was better when I could pronounce 'Gethsemane,'" she said.

"Mom," I told her, "most people who hadn't just had a stroke couldn't pronounce Gethsemane." It was then that I knew her departure might be a long and winding road.

That spring I flew back to meet Pam and move Mom into assisted living, a serene place in downtown Amarillo with a resident cat and dog, as well as the usual bad food and Bingo nights. But the care was exceptional; the nurses loved Ruby, and there was no better place within hundreds of miles. We had each offered to have her live with us—I had a house in Cambridge, Pam in Santa Fe—but it was a gesture full of courtesy and ambivalence on all our parts; we knew she wouldn't come and that she required more physical care than we could provide alone. She wanted to stay in the city she'd lived in for more than sixty years. But on moving day she grew grim and finally mute, refusing to speak to anyone, including the woman who came to greet her or either Pam or me.

My dad had a ritual when I visited of taking me in his office and showing me his stock portfolio, which he had built from nothing over many years of smart choices and nerves of steel. Then he would say the same thing: "If anything happens to me, promise me your mother won't wind up in a nursing home."

This conversation had been taking place

biannually for a decade or two, and by the time my father was in his early eighties, he had the beginnings of Alzheimer's and I had learned to shape my answers into a bearable truth. I had already taken away his driver's license on one terrible day, when I convinced him, finally, to sign a durable power of attorney by saying, "You know I would never hurt you. You know." And so now, faced with this promise so many middle-aged children are asked to make, I said, "I will always take care of her. I promise."

By which I meant I would find her the best care I could, not that I would move her into my apartment in the frigid Northeast and make both of us insane for the last few years of her life. My father's idea of nursing homes was a realistic but apocalyptic one; what he meant was that he didn't want her lost and forgotten in a urine-soaked warehouse. Instead we had found her a beautiful room with her own furniture and twenty-four-hour nursing care, and we hired the woman who had helped her stay at home for years to continue doing her laundry and running errands. Within three weeks of moving there, she loved the place and called it her home, relieved that the task of dismantling her four-bedroom house was now left to her daughters.

She lived another nine months. When I went to visit I would pile on the bed with peanut-butter crackers and a Diet Coke, my mother laughing loyally at the jokes I told that she could barely hear. She had fallen greatly but not without dignity, and now she sat in a wheelchair watching the Food Network, pointing the remote so fiercely at her little thirteen-inch Sony that she looked as though she might shoot the TV if it misbehaved. The nurses adored her, so much so that occasionally they suffered her delusions, like the day she took too much pain medication for her back and became convinced that I had emptied all her bank accounts and gone on the lam. Unaware of any of this, I called from Cambridge to say hello and got a voice from the bottom of a well. "How are you doing, Mom?" I asked.

"Well, I'm fine," she said, her voice suspicious and darkly sarcastic. "The question is, how are *you?*"

It took five minutes of my careful reassurances for her to accept that all was well and that her worries were unfounded. "I dreamed you took all my money and ran off with some sleazy guy in a pickup truck," she said, not yet persuaded that I hadn't, and I started laughing, probably in relief but also because the image seemed hilarious. I'd been in charge of her finances for years, and questionable guys in pickup trucks belonged to the far-distant past.

21.

My mother believed that my independence was inborn and crucial to who I was, and she liked to illustrate this with a story about my sitting on her lap in a rocking chair when I was three or four. "After a little while you'd say, 'I want to get down now, Mother,' " she'd tell me, as if my withdrawal were evidence of the rebel girl to come. It was years before I began to view this as a partly sad image—one that conjures not just pluck but also a kind of restless sorrow. Somewhere between her version and mine, character is born: the map of experience and destiny that evolves into a self.

When she died she cried two tears, and because she had been unconscious for hours and without water for days, the tears were like someone calling from far away. It was a winter evening in 2006, and my fifty-fifth birthday. A few days earlier she had suffered what was probably a silent pulmonary embolism. I flew to Texas and went straight to the hospital from the airport, and when I came into her room she started crying out and reaching for me. That was

167

the last sign my sister and I had that she knew we were there.

We moved her to hospice the next morning—a quiet, soft place marred only by a visit from the on-call physician, who dropped by during the long afternoon. By then she was completely still, a bird waiting for flight, and her body was showing early signs of the dying process. The doctor poked her knees and talked loudly. "These old pioneer women," he said to me and my sister. "It can take them a while to die. I've seen them go ten days without water."

It was such a stupid thing to say, in so many ways, and Pam and I shot a look at each other and told him we could take it from here. But after he left I flew into a panic—a feeling of chaos and urgency that causes my chest to tighten even now. I wanted out of Amarillo: away from this terrible, airless circle of waiting. Away from the grief of burying the last parent. I felt like a sprinter, who thought she could finish the race, only to be told it was a marathon. I knew that I could not bear this for ten days, or even three, and I knew my mother couldn't, either.

The nurse on duty told us that things weren't going to change anytime soon, and so Pam and I left late that afternoon for an hour or so—she to tend to things at my parents' house, which was empty and had been for sale for a couple of months. I drove to the local gym to throw myself in the pool and get a shower. Our plan was to check in by phone and meet back at hospice.

I have always felt guilty about the timing of that swim, even though a larger part of me believes it was the right ending, a script my mother would have approved. While I did laps in the pool I let the hugeness of my mother's dying wash over me, a feeling that could emerge only when the world was quiet. I was coming out of the shower when I heard my cell phone ring inside the locker, and I grabbed it and heard my sister saying, "They just called—we need to get back there now." I threw on my clothes and drove the two miles to hospice and half-ran from the car to the building. I remember the brown sweater I was wearing and how heavy it was because it was damp and how my wet hair felt in the dry Texas cold. I saw my mother's best friend, Hylasue, just inside the door; she was waving for me to hurry.

Pam was already there. I got to the other side of the bed and we leaned over her while our mother reached her whole self upward toward her next breath. It lasted about five minutes. I had my hands on her shoulders, and I saw a tear in the corner of her eye, and then one in the other, and they ran down her cheeks toward her ears like stars exploding. And I said, "Oh, my God, look"—and she took one last breath and then a sound was coming from somewhere and I realized it was me.

I never understood how people were able to write the obituary of a loved one, particularly in that first corridor after death. But the next morning I woke up with a jolt of purpose and sat at the peninsula in my parents' kitchen and wrote the death notice for the local paper. The peninsula was a short counter space at the end of the cooking area that was everyone's favorite spot in the house. I had sat there after I was grown and looked out at the backyard and talked to my mother while she cooked. She was a good cook, patient and modest, and whenever I went home to visit she'd say, "Well, there's nothing to eat," and I'd open the refrigerator. Inside would be baked chicken breasts and fresh fruits and vegetables and maybe some leftover rice or potatoes and some sliced brisket she'd picked up from the best barbecue in Amarillo. And a couple of homemade pies, custard and pecan, on the sideboard.

The peninsula was where Mom had served me BLT sandwiches and hot tea for breakfast when I was a teenager—when I was moody and almost impossible to please. She made them especially for me, because I was skinny and they were the only thing that sounded good. Then thirty years passed and she stood there making oatmeal for my niece, Claire, who loved the seat in the kitchen as much as I did, so much that we fought over it for years until I gave up and tried to be a grown-up about it. But still.

Anyway that was where I wrote the obituary, where I included the fact that Ruby Groves Caldwell had been a star high school basketball player—she was five feet three—but I forgot to mention her decades-long devotion to Westminster Presbyterian Church. Then Pam and I went to the funeral home that had taken care of my dad and I typed up the notice on their old IBM Selectric, because their computers were down and I wanted to make sure they got it right. We already had the Scripture verses that she loved from Ecclesiastes and the psalms, and we needed three hymns, and poring over the hymnbook—accompaniment to so many endless Sunday mornings when we were girls—we started laughing and half-crying and couldn't stop. And finally we chose "Ave Maria," a suspiciously Catholic song for a Protestant congregation, but the song we most loved for my mom.

She was laid out at the funeral home for the next two days, until the service on Monday. The first night she was there we drove over from the house. I had brought from Cambridge a small cloisonné box with a little fawn on it that I wanted to bury with her, and I slipped it inside the fold of her arm. And then Pam said, a little sadly, "She isn't wearing earrings," and I thought it was such a sister thing to say—my sis the fashion plate, who could make a runway item out of a potato sack. Then she said, "I'll be back—I'm going to get her earrings." And she drove across town, eight o'clock on a Saturday night, so tired she didn't even know it yet, and went to my mom's assisted-living facility and found the right earrings and came back in twenty minutes. And placed them on our mother's ears, very gently, and said, "There."

My mom is buried next to my dad, in the Texas sun, with a headstone that gives the year of their births—both 1914—and a ribbon engraved between their names with 1943, the date of their marriage.

We had picked the headstone together, my mother and I, and she had stood there with me the year after my dad died while I tended his grave. I had brought a trowel and a watering can and fresh flowers, and I arranged the flowers while she leaned against a tree. And out of the blue she said to me, "I will *always* be with you."

It was a lovely, comforting thing to say, a moment of something in the middle of nothing, and I reached for it like a little girl, wanting it to last. "Will you?" I said. "Will you stay?" By which I meant, *Thank you, I love you, death is scary.* And she, irritated by my need, said, half impatiently, "Well, I *said* I would."

I had been scheduled to travel that winter, and several weeks after Ruby's death I flew out west, and in airports, when I was waiting for a flight, I found a chair somewhere and wrapped myself in my big winter coat and closed my eyes and rocked. Then I would let myself think, *My mother is dead my mother is dead,* and it became a kind of brutal litany that gave me enough peace to keep me from feeling crazy. Grief on the run. I felt that I'd been robbed of something, had missed the stair-step progression of grief, because when I got home she was still dead and I still couldn't believe it. But that's endemic to grief, I think—the feeling that we haven't quite been able to do it right.

When I asked my mother's minister what he had to say about suffering, how he made sense of it, he smiled and said, "God is love." At the time I thought it was an empty thing to say, glossing over the pain of what I had just witnessed, but I suppose he is right on so many levels: God is love and love is memory, and memory is a bruise or a warmth or a grocery list you cannot bear to throw away.

My mother said to me, "Promise me you won't take a drink after I'm gone."

• • •

She said, "I know how hard it is"—she meant
life, and the usual troubles—and she said, "All I
can tell you is that it gets better."

She said, "Those jeans are too tight.
     "That lipstick is too dark."
She said, "Wouldn't it be nice if we could all be
as smart as you."

22.

....

The heroes far outnumber the villains in this story. The worst culprit here is a virus called poliomyelitis, and I've never taken it personally that I was one of its casualties, any more than I believe that it had me in its sights that summer of 1951. I don't like demonizing disease, as though a bacterium or cell mutation could be capable of malevolent intent. Trees falling and viruses invading and lions stalking prey are not preoccupied with collateral damage on their march through life, however rough it may be on what lies in their path.

People have asked me over the years if I was ever angry about the polio. It seemed an odd question the first time I heard it, and startles me still. That response tells me how fully I've absorbed this piece of the picture into my life story. After all, there were only a few months when I didn't have polio or its consequences, so it is my baseline. The wall you push against. Everybody's got one.

I've also been asked if I was resentful about getting a new diagnosis as late as I did, at least a decade beyond the initial symptoms that indicated my hip was failing. The answer is no, and not because I'm trying to be valiant. I think it's because of all the years I've spent in AA meetings, listening to people's stories. They can be terrible stories, full of anguish and fear and disrepair. But the point is not to spin the narrative; that defeats the purpose, in some way, of story itself. You can't change the tale so that you turned left one day instead of right, or didn't make the mistake that might have saved your life a day later. We don't get those choices. The story is what got you here, and embracing its truth is what makes the outcome bearable.

So—no anger here. I don't get to be mad at a resident or a physical therapist or an internist who was working a twelve-hour day and assumed I needed a cortisone shot or a referral instead of an X-ray. A thousand little subplots converged on the days I didn't get what I needed, and chances are, almost none of them were about me.

But then I found Dr. Ranere and Dr. Mattingly, and all the good people who listened and paid attention and did the right thing. This is what I like to think of as a dramatic shift in the narrative.

I don't believe much in miracles. Too flashy, too little empirical evidence that the glow lasts. Instead I'll take the slower route: an apple a day, a thousand leg lifts. I do think you need to be listening when the thunder cracks, because that way you get to be there for the light show that accompanies it. Then you will have been witness to splendor, and will know how to keep an eye out for it.

I am standing in the foyer of my health club with Chris, a.k.a. Neutrina, a woman of such natural grace and strength that I once told her she reminded me of a tree unfolding. So that became another code name between the two of us—"Tree Unfolding." Because she teaches physics, I've asked her a question about momentum—about why it is that, once you have achieved a certain speed and efficiency while swimming or walking, the momentum itself begins to carry you. I have stumbled upon this accidentally, the way innocents always uncover the earth's obvious truths. It's happened a few times in the boat, and now in the pool, because my leg is strong enough to send me forward. On land it's been a harder victory: too many months of slogging in slow motion, as though I am underwater. A staircase of hope and defeat, hope and defeat. Do that ten thousand times, again and again.

Then one day I tried walking a little faster, and faster made it easier. This puzzles me—in the Law According to Gail, everything is hard and must be earned.

I demonstrate the slow-motion walk for Chris, and then the faster gait. Then she shows me what I've been doing. In my slow, careful walk, she tells me, I am pushing matter sideways, wasting energy. When I speed up, I am doing what walking is: pushing the earth behind me as I go.

Tree Unfolding far prefers the laws of Newton to the laws of Gail. "Touch the world," she tells me, "and it touches you back."

23.

....

Winter 2012–2013

When I came home from the hospital after surgery, Peter had left a welcome sign on my front door that read HIP-HIP HORRAY, YOU ARE HOME. I taped the sign to an inside wall, where I could see it while I did exercises. I love it for a couple of reasons: The *Y* is drawn and decorated in the form of a crutch, and the misspelling of *hooray* is pure Peter—ever the artist and designer, eschewing spelling for image and intent. Yes, I am home, and it can take a long time to know what that means, and to cherish the notion of it.

The year after my mother died, I became embroiled in a property dispute with a neighbor, and for a while I thought I would just pick up and go—leave this neighborhood and these good friends, the parks and bodies of water and familiar faces on the street that make up so much of a life. When I was struggling with the idea, I woke one night with a start and an urgent thought: *If I move, my mother won't know where to find me.* I was so haunted by this conviction that it stayed with me for days, as though I might have pulled up camp and left no note: the passionate, irrational feeling that I was the fixed object now, the earthbound lioness, and she the ethereal soul who needed always to know where I was.

These days I walk a hilly two-mile trail loop in the forests with the dogs, and I do it without fear or even much fatigue. I unnerved Shiloh the other day because I got ahead of what she perceived, with that vigilant sheepdog brain, as being my usual pace. I'm using both legs in the pool, and I finished the rowing season—a tougher season than I had hoped, but one that had its particular joys. For years I had overcorrected as I rowed, using my right arm to do what my leg could not. This year, overcorrecting automatically, I nearly swerved into a sandbar; my right leg was trying to pull its own weight.

Polio-affected muscles and tendons still give me trouble and always will. Camp Gail is open permanently, I suppose. I'll never run a marathon, or even a fifty-yard sprint, but I did do a waltz with the dogs on the pathway at Fresh Pond the other day, just to prove that I could.

I don't know yet what or how much I'll get back. I've passed the crucial year mark, the period most professionals say it takes to fully recover from joint replacement, though my surgeon tells me that's probably only halfway for me. Some days I still feel like the Tin Man, no oilcan in sight, my new and realigned parts adjusting to the reconstructed architecture of my body. Developing a leg at sixty requires more patience and acceptance than doing so at two, or seventeen, or even forty. But I am taller and stronger than I thought I would ever be again, and the hugeness of that trumps how hard it's been to get here.

When I went to see my doctor eight months after surgery, I walked into his office and said, grinning, "I think you should add, to your considerable résumé, 'Cured polio.' " He liked that, though I don't think he needed it—the best surgeons are already pretty happy with what they pull off. He tells me that over time I might recover as much as 85 percent strength in my right leg, a notion that seems astounding. Of course there is the counterforce of time, the forward march of life toward its great shadowy end. I do know that my real challenge is not the leg lifts or the river or the embrace of an unknowable future, but the task of receiving what happened to me as the blessing it is. My rewrite with a happy outcome.

The other thing I know now is that we survive grief merely and surely by outlasting it—the ongoing fact of the narrative eclipses the heartbreak within, a deal that seems to be the price we pay for getting to hold on to our beloved dead. One afternoon at the end of summer, when I was rowing, I started talking to Caroline, upstream by the reeds where I used to watch a muskrat. And I said to her, *Are you there, are you listening?* and tears started streaming down my face, which doesn't happen much to me anymore. I said, "It's just too lonely to think that you're not. I need to think that my dad is still proud of me, and that you still understand me. Just too lonely without that."

And I thought, *Maybe it would be too hard and complicated if you're still there as CK, blond and skinny and laughing, because, let's face it, there have been billions upon billions of people and that's a lot of overload, even for God, that's a lot of two-way cosmic dialogues going on at once. So maybe it's a big huge bowl of Jell-O consciousness, where the individuals connect when they need to. That is what we interpret, earthbound, as memory and love: We are all angels unawares.*

It was ninety degrees and sunny, and suddenly the blue sky darkened and a cool breeze came out of nowhere and gave me about thirty seconds of respite from the heat. And I thought, *Well, what else would they do if they were thinking, "Let's send her a message that we got her message. Let's send her a cool breeze for just a minute"?*

I thought all this between the muskrat and the bridge, and when I rounded the bend I heard Caroline telling me to remember to use my abs during the recovery. Then I rowed another half-mile before I turned at the sandbar and headed home.

In late September I spent a sunny, blustery weekend in Westport, Massachusetts, near the Rhode Island border, where there are coves and causeways and miles of rocky beaches. The last day I was there I drove to the beach in early afternoon, hoping that the crowds might have thinned and that Tula and I could sneak onto the beach. We walked for about a quarter of a mile on a road above the dunes, and then crossed a planked bridge over the rose hips to the beach below. The only people nearby were a couple who had seen the signs in the parking lot—NO DOGS UNTIL NOVEMBER—and were hiding their little black dog under a beach towel. Then they saw Tula and we smiled and waved at each other.

Whenever people ask me where Tula's name comes from, I tell them it's an old Southern name I've always loved. That's only part of the story. I named her after Cyd Charisse, the dancer whose athletic beauty belonged to the era of Fred Astaire and Gene Kelly. When Charisse died in 2008, several people sent me the obituary, because she was born and grew up in Amarillo. One friend added a commentary: "Are all long-legged Texans from Amarillo?" That was how I learned that Charisse was a small-town Texas girl, christened Tula Ellice Finklea, and that she had caught polio when she was six, in the 1920s. Her father, who loved the ballet, sent her to dance lessons to build up her strength, and opened the door to dance history.

So I named my dog after a dancer—probably somewhere knowing that I might bestow her with the physical grace and agency that I lacked but always longed for. My Tula would be a four-legged showgirl, and anyone who has ever seen a Samoyed running through the forest will know that the image is not that far off. When she runs through surf, though, she does a little backward foxtrot and catches herself, then twists to the side and begins again.

At the beach in Westport the tide was coming in and the sun was bright and the water temperature was about sixty-five degrees—an ocean too cold to swim in but too sensual to resist. The shoreline leading up to the water was rocky, treacherously so, with dinosaur egg–size rocks for as far as you could see. I navigated over the rocks in my sneakers, but I stopped when I got to the water's edge, afraid to take off my shoes and go it alone. For years I had mostly slid myself into the ocean, straight from shoes to total immersion, a far better swimmer than walker. I didn't know if I was really able to wade barefoot, and I couldn't remember the last time I'd tried.

And then I thought, *Oh, so what's the worst that will happen—you will fall on this beautiful sand.* So I took off my shoes, and I could walk better than I had in years, and I remembered what it was like to have water running through my toes in the sand. I am Bernadette in ecstasy, wading in the grotto. And the farther I waded, the easier it became, with Tula herding me back and forth, galloping into the surf and out again. I was wading in the September Atlantic and looking ahead and thinking, *Run, Tula Ellice, run past all your sorrows, and dance and keep on going, until we all fall down.*

Acknowledgments

....

I tend to think of memoir as a prism; there is no shining a pure or direct light on the past. My sister, Pamela Caldwell Morrison, has been an ally and a tremendous help in my navigation of memory and narrative. Kate Medina and Lindsey Schwoeri at Random House offered a generous blend of perspective and editorial wisdom; my thanks to them for their guidance. Lane Zachary, my agent and friend, has been the best of both as I have thought my way through the book. Louise Erdrich, Jean Kilbourne, and Andrea Cohen listened, read, buoyed, and consoled; each gave me invaluable creative and emotional support.

Two personal and social histories of polio reached out to me years ago: Kathryn Black's *In the Shadow of Polio* and Jane S. Smith's *Patenting the Sun*. More recently, David M. Oshinsky's *Polio: An American Story* provided what is probably the definitive social history on the U.S. epidemics and the race for a vaccine.

What I've learned about dogs over the past two decades has come greatly from the dogs them-selves. Humans have helped, too, and my particular thanks for their acuity and instruction to Peter Wright, Amy Kantor, Marjorie Gatchell, Dorothy Gracey, Kathy de Natale, and Janice Hovelmann.

A number of friends gave freely of their kindness, forbearance, and splendid humor; I came through the past few years in their good company. My gratitude and love to Penny Potter, Nancy Hays, Peter and Pat Wright, Donna Warner, Tink and David Davis, Chris Pasterczyk, Avery Rimer, Rocco Ricci, Peter James, Jill and Marc Schermerhorn, Morgan McVicar, and the women at the M.A.C. My special thanks for taking care of me to Stephen Ranere, MD, and David A. Mattingly, MD.

Finally, two pillars of strength. The indomitable spirit of my mother, Ruby Caldwell, hovers throughout this book; several years after her death, she gives me courage to this day. So does Dick Chasin, who has helped me learn to walk in every sense. That's why this book is dedicated to him.

About the Author

....

Gail Caldwell is the author of two previous memoirs, *Let's Take the Long Way Home* and *A Strong West Wind.* The former chief book critic for *The Boston Globe*, she received the Pulitzer Prize for distinguished criticism in 2001. Caldwell lives in Cambridge, Massachusetts.

Center Point Large Print
600 Brooks Road / PO Box 1
Thorndike ME 04986-0001 USA

(207) 568-3717

US & Canada:
1 800 929-9108
www.centerpointlargeprint.com